ENDORSEMENTS

"Pastor Kristina Burroughs just gave aspiring and current female leaders a catapult forward with her new book, The Most Important Yes. Kristina's articulation of principles and practices to ascend above those things in our lives that sabotage our Divine Design and potential will provide much needed depth and understanding any leader needs to be successful both in life and calling."
   -Dr. Mike Cuckler, Chair of SEU School of Divinity

"I have had the honor of watching, praying, coaching, and advising Kristina through key transitional challenges that are unique to strong and gifted women leading authentically while loving God and their families passionately. The voice you will recognize in this read will settle your often unspoken yearning and heart cry for the callings that you cannot ignore. Wisdom, understanding, motivation, and compassion are wrapped in these anointed chapters and questions."
   -Dr. Joseph Umidi, EVP Regent University

"Kristina's book is a field manual filled with practical wisdom for women who want to live in all God has available for them. By weaving personal stories of overcoming obstacles with the basic truths in the word of God, you will find yourself inspired, challenged and strengthened to live out a life that says "yes" to what God is leading you to do. You will discover you are not alone and that your "yes" plays a significant part in the story God is writing over humanity at this time in history!"
   -Dr. Donna Pisani, Pastor & Author

"Kristina uses her life experience, the ups and the downs, to encourage and inspire women to keep pursuing God, to keep going forward in discovering all that God has for them and wants to do through them! You will love relating with some of the pitfalls and challenges, as well as the victories and the beauty discovered along the way to saying yes to God and trusting Him in that process."
   -Lora Batterson, National Community Church

Having had the great joy and honor to cross paths with Kristina Burroughs and being a witness to her faithful and courageous walk with her LORD and Savior, I recommend this book to all my sisters in the LORD and those still on their journey toward Him. Her authenticity in recounting her own journey of faith invites us all to courageously trust and embrace God's plan for our lives, regardless of the cost, regardless of the detours, regardless... What a great and inspiring read!
   -Dr. Doris Gomez, Dean School of Business and Leadership,
   Regent University

"This book is for every woman—seeking to know God's plan for their lives and leadership. And for every man—who knows a woman!—to understand the unique nature of what it means to be a woman after God's heart. After reading this you will be glad God made you a woman! The reflective sections at the end of chapters is for you to see yourself, learn, and then see yourself again in God's eyes. Kristina details how from the first 'yes' to all the others—we see GOD in it all—and He is with us in pain and joy. This book will encourage you in your faith walk, and if you are questioning your calling, searching for it—this book will draw you closer to all God has for you."

-Dr. Kathleen Patterson, Director,
Doctorate of Strategic Leadership Program, Regent University

THE MOST IMPORTANT YES

Womanhood from a God-Centered Perspective

KRISTINA JOWERS BURROUGHS

WESTBOW
PRESS®
A DIVISION OF THOMAS NELSON
& ZONDERVAN

Copyright © 2024 Kristina Jowers Burroughs.

All rights reserved. No part of this book may be used or reproduced by any means, graphic, electronic, or mechanical, including photocopying, recording, taping or by any information storage retrieval system without the written permission of the author except in the case of brief quotations embodied in critical articles and reviews.

This book is a work of non-fiction. Unless otherwise noted, the author and the publisher make no explicit guarantees as to the accuracy of the information contained in this book and in some cases, names of people and places have been altered to protect their privacy.

WestBow Press books may be ordered through booksellers or by contacting:

WestBow Press
A Division of Thomas Nelson & Zondervan
1663 Liberty Drive
Bloomington, IN 47403
www.westbowpress.com
844-714-3454

Because of the dynamic nature of the Internet, any web addresses or links contained in this book may have changed since publication and may no longer be valid. The views expressed in this work are solely those of the author and do not necessarily reflect the views of the publisher, and the publisher hereby disclaims any responsibility for them.

Any people depicted in stock imagery provided by Getty Images are models, and such images are being used for illustrative purposes only.
Certain stock imagery © Getty Images.

Scripture quotations taken from The Holy Bible, New International Version® NIV® Copyright © 1973 1978 1984 2011 by Biblica, Inc. TM. Used by permission. All rights reserved worldwide.

Scripture taken from The Message. Copyright © 1993, 1994, 1995, 1996, 2000, 2001, 2002. Used by permission of NavPress Publishing Group.

ISBN: 978-1-9736-9946-0 (sc)
ISBN: 978-1-9736-9947-7 (hc)
ISBN: 978-1-9736-9941-5 (e)

Library of Congress Control Number: 2023909785

Print information available on the last page.

WestBow Press rev. date: 03/04/2024

To women who have decided to follow Christ and who struggle to trust God in the process of walking out his plan for their lives

I wrote this book so that women and my daughters, Hanna and Abigail, will be inspired to run their race well that God has laid out for them.

CONTENTS

Foreword ix
Acknowledgments xi
Introduction xiii

1. Your First Yes. 1
2. The Process. 10
3. Fear into Faith 15
4. Not Every Opportunity Is a God Door. 20
5. Yielding to His Lead 25
6. Confronting Competition and Comparison 33
7. Unpacking Your Yesterdays. 39
8. Letting Go of Control 46
9. Weeding the Garden 51
10. Through the Valley. 57
11. At the Crossroads. 63
12. Hope and New Life 69
13. Hindrances, Lies, and Transformation 75
14. Fear Is a Liar 85
15. Tackling Shame Head-On 89
16. Control versus Surrender 95
17. Trust and Healing 100
18. The Waiting and Reward. 110

FOREWORD

I love leadership books written by those who have actually led—through highs and lows, through thick and thin. I've had a front row seat as Kristina and Jeremy Burroughs planted Catalyst Church. In fact, I have the joy of being an overseer. One thing is certain: God's favor is on their life and leadership.

This book may be printed with ink, but it's written with blood, sweat, and tears. As you read, you'll identify with the unique challenges of leadership. It's not for the faint of heart. It will also give you the courage to continue your leadership journey.

Every journey begins with one little yes. Like a single domino that creates a domino effect, the first domino is often the hardest to push over. Why? It takes the most faith. But faith is taking the first step before God reveals the second step. And that first step has a way of turning into a giant leap.

There are no shortcuts or cheat codes when it comes to leadership! And for women, it can be more of an uphill climb. But I love the way Kristina says this: "God made no mistake making you a woman." Permission to speak frankly? I believe men and women are equally called to lead, but I think women have a unique advantage. What is that secret bullet? Women have a larger corpus collosum—the interhemispheric connection between the right and left brain. In other words, women tend to have greater fluidity between the logical left brain and creative right brain.

In my opinion, when it comes to leadership, authenticity is authority. There are no perfect leaders. There are only those who are courageous enough to own their mistakes and admit them to others. I don't trust leaders who pretend to walk on water. I trust those who lead with a limp.

I appreciate the vulnerability that Kristina shares in these pages. You'll find plenty of identification points.

There never has been and never will be anyone like you. That isn't a testament to you. It's a testament to the God who created you. The significance of that is this: no one can lead like you or for you. And it always starts with the first yes!

Legacy is not what you accomplish. Legacy is what others accomplish because of you. Therein lies the challenge. As Kristina says: "Know this: your agreement carries weight in God's eyes for future generations." May this book unleash a generational blessing in your life and leadership.

Mark Batterson

ACKNOWLEDGMENTS

I credit my husband, Jeremy Burroughs, for our three beautiful children, Hanna, Judah, and Abigail. I thank him for his encouragement and investment in seeing this dream come true. We planted Catalyst Church in January 2019 in Bethesda, Maryland, and work together building God's kingdom in all the ways God leads us to do; we follow his lead in the various seasons of life.

I thank my mother, who exemplified unconditional love, sacrifice, and support. As I raise strong-willed daughters myself, I am even more grateful for all my mother invested in my life. She modeled nurture and what it meant to live out the calling of motherhood.

I thank my stepmother, who taught me how to have grit, to pray, and to get things done! She taught me how to anchor myself to the Word of God as my true north and stay the course, no matter what. She modeled the way of doing hard things with unwavering faith and trust in God, including loving me as her own.

I thank my father for his continued belief, support, and provision as I grew through many phases of immaturity into womanhood. I have never doubted for a moment how much my father loved me, even though I did not live with him full time. He relentlessly took every moment to teach virtues and character, which have guided my life. He taught me how to believe God for the impossible and to never stop dreaming.

I thank my stepfather for modeling a high value on education and seeking knowledge to make informed decisions and opinions about life. My value for education and continued learning has led me to write this book as a catalyst to help you in your spiritual-formation journey.

I honor my sister friends, Summer Mobley, Andrea Hess, Sandhia Rajan, and Linda Phiri, who reviewed this book in its very raw stages and gave me feedback early in the process to make it better before releasing it to you.

I thank Cara Reiter for her encouragement in keeping this book moving forward to encourage others in their faith walk as women.

I thank Mark Batterson for an encouraging word to finish this book and for giving me wisdom for moving forward.

I thank Lora Batterson for who she is in my life and her encouragement as a spiritual mentor and friend.

INTRODUCTION

I wrote this book to affirm your calling, as a woman, as a coheir with Christ. God has a unique purpose and plan for your life. He made no mistake by making you a woman. God has called you, anointed you, and will empower you to be a light for him in what can seem like a dark world. You are a solution-carrier, and God chose to display hope through you—yes, you!

Walking with God does not promise that all of your dreams will come true in the way you think they will. Walking with God does not guarantee that your goals and timelines will be met in the way you want them. Walking with God *does* guarantee a hope and a future beyond anything you can imagine, but it will take a lifetime to walk out. It also will take holding on to his promises when you experience quite the opposite in your situation.

Nevertheless, we pray, "Thy Kingdom come, thy will be done here on earth as it is in heaven!" This prayer requires a complete surrender of what we had in mind.[1] It requires an honest look at our false selves,[2] unhealed wounds,[3] and underlying lies[4] that may be operating under the surface of our lives, as well as the choice to turn away from the modern-day idols that war for first place in our hearts.

As an organizational leadership graduate and someone who is absolutely fascinated with assembling teams and moving groups of people toward a

---

[1] *New International Life Application Version* (Carol Stream, IL: Tyndale House Publishing, 2019).
[2] P. Scazzero, *Emotionally Healthy Spirituality* (Grand Rapids, MI: Zondervan, 2017), 39.
[3] K. & M. Luse, *Connect Up Healing Prayer Ministry Training Manual* (Harrisburg, PA: Connect Up Ministry, 2018).
[4] C. & B. Kylstra, *Restoring the Foundations* (Mount Juliet, TN: Restoring the Foundations International, 2001).

mission worth advancing, I have found that the ways of the kingdom often counter the cultural norms of our day. We must willingly choose to take up the cross of servant leader and daughter of the most high God as our highest calling, often against the current cultural trends. God's ways are certainly not our ways, and I'm grateful for that. If I had my way, I would have missed out on the richest blessings in this life to date because they were not in my plan. I would have completely bypassed all the hard places where my character was formed and the real fruit of God's spirit was grown in the dark. Now, as a wife and mother, the four other people who live with me have refined and matured me in ways I didn't even know I needed. God uses the weak areas of our lives to reveal himself the most. In our struggles, we find treasures that cannot be found any other way, and we can experience the fullness of joy that comes from submitting to God's plan for our lives.

Through my personal story and the power of a simple yes, I hope to debunk some lies that you may have heard and to reveal some powerful truths about walking in your true identity as a daughter of Christ. Your story is important. As you read the words on these pages, I pray that God will speak clearly and powerfully to you about your own journey and show you that he has been and is with you every step of the way. I pray that he will speak to you about your next *yes*. He wants you to trust him with your life at every crossroad. As you read with an open heart and a willingness to follow his lead, I believe this book will catapult you into your next step in your journey, serving as a catalyst for needed change.

My heart for you is that you will not approach this book as something to be accomplished but that you'll read slowly and contemplatively for transformation. I implore you to practice the spiritual disciplines of silence, solitude, and reflection with God as you read.[5] There is no deadline or review due date at the end of this book, so take your time. This book is an invitation to journey with God right where you are and to intentionally position your heart to listen to what he says to you through my own story and yours.

Pause at the end of each chapter and use the reflection questions there.[6] Yes, it is OK to write on the pages and make it your own experience! I

---

[5] Richard Foster, *The Celebration of Discipline* (New York, NY: Harper Collins, 1978).
[6] John Orthberg, *The Life You've Always Wanted* (Grand Rapids, MI: Zondervan, 2015).

added the reflection section for all of my sisters who struggle to pick up blank pages of a journal and for those who love to write in the margins of books. If you don't put what you read into practice immediately, this book will become another accomplishment, rather than a catalyst for transformation. Choose the catalyst. You are already well accomplished, sister! If God speaks clearly to you about some area, take a moment to surrender that area or to take the action he prompts you to take. My dear friend Dr. Julie Reams says, "God reveals what he wants to heal." By this, you will be a doer of the Word, not just a hearer, as you exercise your faith muscles![7]

My prayer for you is that by reading this story of my life and what God has taught me along my journey, you will realize the power of giving a single *yes* to God. You are one decision away from a totally different life!

---

[7] James 1:22.

CHAPTER 1

Your First Yes

As a thirteen-year-old child at youth camp, I can remember sitting around a campfire and singing a song to Jesus. That night, I made a commitment to God that has forever marked my life. It was the first time I thought I understood the weight of this decision, and I knew it would shape every decision from that point forward. While I'd grown up in church, I made a decision that night to genuinely commit my whole life to God and follow his lead. I had no idea that decision would mark the rest of my days so significantly. I had no idea of the power of my yes that night. The stars were bright and the moon was shining as I stared into the campfire while our youth pastor encouraged us to spend some time with God and to listen. For the first time ever, I discerned the voice of God. I heard a small whisper in my heart and mind, reciting Isaiah 6:5–9. That night, I answered what I perceived to be a call to go to the nations and share the good news.

> Then one of the angel-seraphs flew to me. He held a live coal that he had taken with tongs from the altar. He touched my mouth with the coal and said, "Look. This coal has touched your lips, Gone your guilt, your sins wiped out." And then I heard the voice of the Master, "Whom shall I send? Who will go for us?" I spoke up, "I'll go. Send me!" (Isaiah 6:5–9 MSG)

I remember an excitement that infiltrated my heart as I finally recognized God's voice, the same one I had learned about in Sunday school all of my life! It became a profoundly personal relationship that night, and I held on to what I heard him whisper to me about my destiny. I pondered it from that day forward, often trying to rush ahead, make things happen, and do it myself. The God of the universe spoke to me, and I heard him! I often think of the mother of Jesus, Mary, and the power of her agreement to accept the call to raise Jesus and groom him for his ultimate assignment. That thirteen-year-old girl simply believed what the angel of the Lord told her, and it changed the entire course of her life; she raised the Son of God.

> "I am the Lord's servant," Mary answered. "May your word to me be fulfilled." Then the angel left her. (Luke 1:38 NIV)

We stand on the shoulders and walk in the shoes of many biblical women of faith who have gone before us. They, too, clung to their most important promise to trust God in their lives. Sarah, the great matriarch of our faith, along with her husband, Abraham, trusted God and left comfort to follow God into a land he would show them. She messed up along the way and made some poor decisions, but God still used her in a powerful way. Aren't you glad? That means that we, too, have a chance to be used mightily by God in all of our mistakes and missteps.[8] Hannah contended for the desires that God put in her heart for a child. She pressed into God, remembering her agreement to trust God despite her delayed promises. She eventually gave birth to Israel's first prophet, Samuel, who anointed Israel's greatest king and played a significant role in Israel's history. She could have given up when it got tough, but she chose to keep her promise to God.[9] Deborah, one of the most influential women of the Bible, led an army courageously during a time of war and recommitted her promise to God, trusting that he was enough to lead her army to victory.[10]

Elizabeth, John the Baptist's mother, was bold enough to embrace motherhood and humiliation, as her husband went mute after encountering an angel of the Lord, believing this child was a special gift from God and a forerunner for Jesus himself.[11] Mary Magdalene honored her radical

---

[8] Genesis 12–17.
[9] 1 Samuel 1:1–28.
[10] Judges 4:8–10.
[11] Luke 1:5–25.

promise to Jesus even after his death. She was the first to see Jesus and tell the other disciples that Christ had risen; in doing so, she became the first evangelist.[12] Phoebe, Johanna, Lydia, and Susanna were women followers of Jesus who also honored their promises to be his messengers in a time when women were not seen as qualified to follow Jesus. Yet they courageously clung to the cause of Christ, honoring their most important promise as examples to the women who would follow in their footsteps. We, dear sister, are those women!

Corrie Ten Boom courageously honored God with her convictions by helping her family to hide Jews in her home during the Nazi Holocaust of World War II. Elizabeth Elliott, a missionary, honored God with her promise to stay behind to minister and be a light of the gospel to the Ecuadorian tribe that killed her husband. Susanna Wesley, the mother of John and Charles Wesley and known as the mother of Methodism, never preached a sermon, yet she raised children who would shape Christian history as we know it. She honored her promise to God in private devotion and prayer that shaped the hearts and lives of her children at home. Jarena Lee honored her promise to God to preach against popular culture in the African Methodist Episcopalian (AME) Church. She was an advocate for women's rights to preach and honored God's call on her life in both the gender and color of his choice. This was not an easy call or road to walk.[13] Rosa Parks, a faithful Christian, honored God by honoring herself as a woman of color, just as God made her, by refusing to move from her seat on a bus, starting a revolution.

Catherine Booth honored her promise to God by cofounding the Salvation Army, and she dedicated her life as a female evangelist to advocating for women's rights in ministry and for those in poverty. Fanny Crosby is best known for honoring God with her yes by composing music, even though she was blind. The road was not easy, yet she honored God with the best that she had to offer despite the hardships. She is best known for writing eight thousand hymns that shaped and influenced Christianity. What might God do with your most important yes?

When life begins to feel boring or mundane, or the enemy—and

---

[12] Luke 8:1–2; Mark 16:1–12.
[13] "6 Christian Women Who Changed the World," Crosswalk.com, accessed April 8, 2022, https://www.crosswalk.com/faith/women/6-christian-women-who-changed-the-world.html.

yes, we have one—begins to sow doubt into the dreams in my heart, I remind myself of the call and the promise I made around the campfire almost thirty years ago! I gave Jesus my yes. No matter how hard it gets or how directionless I have felt in certain seasons of suffering, I have always returned to that conversation I had with God that night. After many wrestling matches and running from God, I eventually surrendered. As daughters, there are additional layers of lies uniquely formed to keep us from becoming all God has called us to be. We have to fight to discover the truth of what God had in mind when he decided to call us female and become a radiant reflection of the love of God to the world around us with his help! There is a history dating back to the garden of Eden, Jewish law, and even Greek and Roman philosophers that has influenced the Western world with underpinning, ungodly beliefs about what it means to be women. After my forty years of life thus far and wrestling with my own calling, I can confidently encourage you, as a woman called by God, to make a difference in the world, but it will not be without a fight. We do not fight against flesh and blood but rather principalities and powers in heavenly places. Many women have fought to pave a way for you and me and won, so it is time to pick up the baton and keep pressing forward for the next generation.

We are in no way second-rate citizens in the kingdom of God, nor are we inferior to males. In fact, the Bible refers to God's creating a suitable helper for Adam called woman. The Hebrew word for helper in this passage is *ezer*, which means "help or assistance."[14] This word is the same word used for the Holy Spirit, as the helper in our lives. The psalmist David actually referred to the Lord as his help. We, too, are referred to in this same manner, as helpers to men. As God's daughters, we are called to be coheirs on the earth as he intended. As a young teenage girl, I heard what I perceived to be God's voice in my heart. I wrestled with it for years because I was not confident this could be true of me as a daughter. I write to you now in complete confidence this was for me, and it is for you too! I write to you now because God desires for his daughters to walk in freedom, confidently passing the baton forward to the next generation. It is time!

Here is what I have come to understand about God's promises: We do

---

[14] L. Cunningham and D. J. Hamilton, *Why Not Women?* (Seattle: YWAM Publishing, 2000), 95–97.

not know or get to decide how or when those promises will come to pass. The only thing we get to decide is whether we will be faithful to our yes in the process, no matter how long it takes. The life of a disciple of Jesus is marked by long obedience in the same direction.[15] Life is a process, and no woman—or man, for that matter—escapes some kind of human suffering or process of sanctification. It is through the process of staying committed to your yes and following God's lead that you will mature and become *more like him*. I emphasized "more like him" because it is important to know that no matter how long you walk with God, you will never be perfect like him. I feel the need to encourage you that no matter how hard you try, you are not him. It's OK!

I can be my hardest critic and have learned to make sure I am not holding myself up to an impossible measuring stick, like being perfect.[16] If that's your goal, you'll fall short every time. This is grace. God looks at a person's heart, not his or her outward résumé. In fact, as we are reminded in Romans 3:11, "There is no one righteous, not even one." I write this to remind the achieving go-getter types that the goal is not perfection.[17] In fact, know this: it is through our weakness that God's power is made strong. While I cringe to write these words, it is the kingdom truth. The key to being strong women of faith is embracing our weakness and understanding that our yes does not mean flawlessness or perfection. It actually means that we will need to make the decision to lay down our need for control and perfection because we know and understand we are safe to follow his lead. God has a history of using imperfect women just like you and me. He is looking for surrender and a willingness to give him your full yes! I can assure you the adventure into which he is inviting you will be well worth the suffering of learning to let go of your plans to embrace him.

As women, the need to control is not unique to any one of us. In fact, the need to control started with the fall in the garden of Eden. The first woman ever created out of a man to complement him began a competition with him. We see that the first mother was tempted with pride from the outset. She took a bite of fear that God might be holding out on her, and

---

[15] Eugene Peterson, *A Long Obedience in the Same Direction* (Downers Grove, IL: InterVarsity Press, 1980).
[16] S. Niequist, *Present over Perfect* (Grand Rapids, MI: Zondervan, 2016).
[17] E. Ley, *Grace, Not Perfection* (Nashville, TN: Thomas Nelson, 2016).

rebellion entered the picture.[18] She entertained doubt and opened the door for all of us to wrestle with control issues. Shame says, "I am not good enough. I fear that if I don't take matters into my own hands and control the outcome, then I will get hurt or miss out." The lies that came into Eve's heart with the first bite came down the bloodline naturally. The good news is that Jesus came to redeem us from the curse and punishment for Eve's sin, which is also ours.

God sent his Son, Jesus, to take the wrath and punishment for sin so that we could be empowered with hope to overcome the lies of the enemy and reverse the curse. I wish I could say that it is that easy, but it is not. We are her daughters, and true freedom never comes without choice. Jesus made a way for us to learn a higher way of living that does not include living in a place of shame, fear, and control.[19] While we all fight the enemy in this way, those with personalities that lend themselves toward directive personality characteristics will struggle all the more. I am speaking from experience. Mainstream culture has not helped us women to find our God-given place as strong women who can simultaneously nurture our homes and lead organizations; these two things seem diametrically opposed. If God is calling you to both, trust him with your promise to work out the details in every season.

As a child of the 1980s, I grew up drinking the Kool-Aid of confusion on a woman's role in American society. The enemy has been after women since the beginning of time. The enemy has sought to oppress, abuse, and enslave women under the hand of our brothers ever since. The apple turned out to be the catalyst that revealed the enemy's hand as he sewed iniquity between the male and female relationship, which caused strife from the start. The enemy has had it out for us women since the onslaught in the garden because we give birth to God's human likeness and are great influencers of his kingdom on earth. We choose to use our influence in partnership with fear and control or faith and submission to God's ways and his plans for our lives. As women, whether or not we have given birth, we have a calling to nurture, lead, and develop people all around us, pointing them to the heart of our Father. As Adam's companion and

---

[18] M. Kassain & N. D. Demoss, *True Womanhood 101: Divine Design* (Chicago, IL: Moody Publishers, 2012).

[19] C. & B. Kylstra, *Restoring the Foundations* (Mount Juliet, TN: Restoring the Foundations International, 2001).

helper, God's intent was that we would make the world a better place as we freely lend our gifts, talents, and hearts to the world around us.

Know this: your agreement carries weight in God's eyes for future generations, not just through the children you raise. As you mature in your relationship with God, you will understand the cost of that agreement. And yes, this will cost everything you have, yet in the end, you'll gain far more than it cost. When I walked down the aisle as a bride of twenty-eight years old, my father, a former law enforcement officer, whispered, "Are you sure you want to do this? I have a getaway car out back!" I clutched his arm as tightly as I could, and, while I was trembling, I took the leap of faith to marriage. What my father knew but I did not fully understand was that this decision would cost me greatly, just as it would benefit me. It would impact the rest of my life. When we say yes to follow Jesus, we say no to all our other lovers and options. We give him all of us and give him permission to lead us however and wherever he chooses. I am convinced we don't always understand the cost of our initial yes, much like I did not understand when I said, "I do." We often struggle because we want Jesus, but we also want to lead ourselves into what we want and think is best for us. If you enter marriage that way—and many of us do—it will cause strife, stress, and discord. Our *yes* means that we will follow God's lead and submit to his lead. This simply means we choose to willingly get under his mission for our lives, even if we are afraid,[20] and it does not look anything like we thought it would look.

Ladies, the consent of many women who have gone before us changed history, as did ours, but it looked vastly different than they imagined it would. Jesus met Mary Magdalene at the tomb and instructed her to go and tell. She did not allow the cultural norms of her day to hold her back. She forged forward with a yes to Jesus to tell her brothers about Jesus's Resurrection. The woman who washed Jesus's feet with her hair boldly came to him, addressing him as rabbi, which was completely countercultural for her day. She prophetically anointed Jesus before his death with perfume that scholars believe would have cost her a year's wages. Her consent to worship Jesus against all odds made it into one of the most popular historical books ever written, the Bible. Deborah said yes to leading an army into battle and fighting for her country's freedom. Phoebe risked her

---

[20] J. Meyer, *Do It Afraid* (Nashville, TN: Faith Words, 2020).

life to take the written gospel letters from Paul to church planters in other cities at a time when women did not do those types of things. Florence Nightingale was convinced of her calling as a God-fearing nurse with a devotion to care for the sick.[21] Her *yes* led her to start hospitals. Many of the first missionaries were women who went to remote and dangerous places to share the gospel. Many go unnamed and are unpopular to us today.[22] Their bold yes changed history and advanced the kingdom of God for eternity.

You're a part of a tribe of women who stand on the shoulders of many who have gone before you, paving a way and setting examples of what it looks like to surrender your life to the *yes* of God's call that leads you and each of us in very different directions.[23] You are not alone. The baton is handed to you in this generation. You get to decide what you will do with it.

Make It Personal

Has your life unfolded the way you thought it would? Take some time to reflect on where you are and where you thought you would be.

_____

_____

_____

If not, what specifically has not worked out the way you thought or has surprised you? Are you glad your plans didn't work out in a certain area? Is there an area for which you still struggle to accept about where you are today? An essential step to moving ahead is acknowledging where you are.

_____

_____

---

[21] "Florence Nightingale," History, updated March 9, 2022, https://www.history.com/topics/womens-history/florence-nightingale-1.

[22] L. Cunningham & D. J. Hamilton, *Why Not Women?* (Seattle, WA: YWAM Publishing, 2000).

[23] "She Rises," accessed on March 1, 2021, http://sherises.com/sheleads.

THE MOST IMPORTANT YES

Take a moment before moving to the next chapter to talk honestly with God right here in the book. You may want to write a letter to God and give him your disappointments. Consider renewing your first commitment to him again by giving him your *yes* again.

_____

_____

_____

_____

_____

_____

CHAPTER 2

The Process

While our first yes sets us on a lifelong journey of learning to follow God's lead, the first yes also sets us on a life trajectory. I have found that it is easy to say yes to a lot of things without completely understanding the weight of my words to God. When I finally said yes to marriage, I understood that decision would automatically mean *no* to any other men for the rest of my life. That was a daunting thought at first, and then it brought incredible security and sacredness to that decision. I waited a long time to say "I do" because I knew how weighty that decision was. I wasn't sure if I was mature enough to handle that kind of yes. That yes only came as a result of my first consent to God. He brought my husband into my life, and as I continued to honor my first yes, God led me to the second most important decision in my life.

I wish that our first yes to God meant that there was no struggle in surrender, but it doesn't. I've learned to give God all of my heart, not just the parts over which I felt comfortable relinquishing control, and I've found it to be the most rewarding relationship of my life. Most of the hard yeses in my life have required me to do it while afraid. The times that I've found exhilarating in my life always required me to "do it afraid."[24]

I stood in front of my small high school graduating class with the opportunity to charge my fellow students with a parting speech on graduation day. I was full of possibility, wonder, and excitement for

---

[24] J. Meyer, *Do It Afraid* (Nashville, TN: Faith Words, 2020), 16.

exploring the world and finding my place in it. I wanted to make a difference. I gave my class a charge from Matthew 7:13–14:

> Enter through the narrow gate. For wide is the gate and broad is the road that leads to destruction, and many enter through it. But small is the gate and narrow the road that leads to life, and only a few find it.

Little did I know how challenging it would be to walk out that charge. I was so busy searching for the narrow road that I became confused. I came to the conclusion that I had to figure it out on my own. The only thing I was ever sure about was my love for God. I had no idea what that expression of love and my gifts would look like, but I was determined to figure it out in my own strength. That road led me to the end of myself many times.

After graduating with a BA in business, I had absolutely no clue what I was going to do with my degree so I continued an entrepreneurial approach of trying things until I figured it out. I searched high and low, from sea to shining sea—literally. That pursuit of many office jobs with no meaningful purpose, tied to the vision and mission of various organizations, left me bored to tears. Then my ambitious pursuit took me on an adventure that eventually led me to a crucible in my relationship with God. I got a job as an activities mate (cruise director) on a small tall ship in the Atlantic Ocean and Caribbean Sea. I got on the airplane with my leather-bound journal; I was in pursuit of my calling with my usual do it myself attitude. I was not sure what I was supposed to do with my life. I had not forgotten the conversation I had under the stars at youth camp, but I was convinced I had to figure this one out on my own. I asked God to make it clear on this adventure. I had no idea that my question and the promise I'd made only eight years earlier were linked.

I have always been a strong-willed redhead, and while that has served me well in most seasons of my life, it has also caused years of needless wandering and internal struggle. I wore myself out, only to find myself right back in the same place I'd left. Perhaps you've heard the story about Moses and the children of Israel. Moses led the people of Israel out of slavery in Egypt but because of their murmuring and complaining, they wandered in circles. They questioned God's ability to provide and lead. They chose to hold on to their ways of thinking that they had learned while in slavery in Egypt. This slavery represented bondage and the "old woman" that strives in her own strength. The escape from Egypt took a lot longer than it needed to take because of their inability to trust God's leading![25] The process of maturity takes time; it will not be rushed. Relationships take time and intentionality, and through that, trust is built. Our relationship with God is similar. We learn to trust him over time as he shows up over and over in our lives in the simplest yet most grandiose ways. We must learn to trust God for the next step, even when we can't always see the whole staircase.

As I boarded the airplane bound for Trinidad, where the tall ship was docked, I was full of both excitement and fear. While I had grown up going on many international mission trips, I'd never left on my own for employment. These were the days before cell phones, and as a young college graduate at the ripe age of twenty-one, I innocently had no real grit for the real world outside the protection of my family. As I reflect on this adventure, I see that while my heart and intent of finding God and finding further clarity on my vocational calling was so right, my own will and desire led me to this tall ship. Yet God met me there, reminding me of my first real yes.

After landing in Trinidad for training, I jumped into the cab of a driver named Jonah, and I encountered God's pursuit like I'd never noticed before. Jonah turned around, and his first words were, "Young lady, why are you running from God? Where are you going?"

I was in shock and hardly said a word the rest of the ride. My first assignment as a seafarer-in-training was training at the docks of Trinidad shipyard; I stayed at a bed-and-breakfast hostel. The woman who ran the hostel had a young teenage daughter who showed me to my room, where I would spend an entire month searching for answers. I thought, *I signed up to lead people to have fun, not firefighting school.* I was the only woman in the class and, out of sheer terror, I begged God for his protection as I was harassed throughout the entire class.

The stress of the situation drove me to find a little church that was having a revival service with a Canadian traveling evangelist. I was hoping

---

[25] Exodus 15–17.

to slip in the back to find some hope and encouragement from what I would call my *embassy*, and I got so much more! They sat me on the front row as a guest, which was not my choice. I intended to leave when I was ready and planned my escape for most of the message. As I determined to leave halfway through the message, the preacher looked straight at me and spoke to my future. He told me things only God knew about me, and he spoke to this future and mission I was desperately trying to figure out for my life. At that moment, I knew God was with me in this process, and he was taking me up on my first promise. I was relieved that God still knew my location, and the God who was with me in the United States was the same God in Trinidad. He went to great lengths to send two complete strangers, only a month after I left home, to remind me of his commitment to me. I thought my *yes* was enough and that I had to figure out the rest on my own. I continued my journey.

I dreamed of traveling internationally and doing something with my gifts and talents that really mattered, so I made it happen. In retrospect, I'm not convinced that God had this job in mind, but it is clear to me now that he turned what the enemy meant for evil and confusion into my good. He met me there on the Caribbean Sea, and I learned to trust my Savior. I experienced God's Word alive in my life and started to understand the extent of the Father's love for me, as he followed me all the way to Trinidad to remind me of my covenant with him.

> Where can I go from your Spirit? Where can I flee from your presence? If I go up to the heavens, you are there. If I make my bed in the depths, you are there. If I rise on the wings of the dawn, if I settle on the far side of the sea, even there your hand will guide me, your right hand will hold me fast. If I say, "Surely the darkness will hide me and the light will become night around me," even the darkness will not be dark to you; the night will shine like the day, for darkness is as light to you. (Psalm 139:7–10 NIV)

This journey is for a lifetime, sister! Stop trying to race to the finish line or worrying if you'll miss it. Stop beating yourself up for detours and trust that God has been and always will be weaving your story for his glory! It will take the entirety of our lives to walk out this process called sanctification and to walk in the fullness of all that God has called us to walk out. Relax a little. Our first yes simply gets the ball rolling, and then we pass through many stages of our faith journeys. We remind ourselves of the first yes, which includes discovering who we are and how God has wired us for his purposes. We accept our God-given limitations,[26] process our experiences, and allow others close enough to sharpen our rough edges through community. We work through our inner layers of protection and woundedness to walk in greater levels of freedom and learn to hear God for ourselves, while submitting to the others he puts in our lives to pace the journey.[27]

Make It Personal

Have you ever tried to make something happen on your own or taken matters into your own hands? How did it go? Have you ever stopped to think how God has shown up in your life, even when you didn't realize it? Daughter, you are loved. God has always been and is in the process with you. There is not a day that he's left you, even in your wandering. There is no limit to how far he'll go to pursue your heart. Take a moment to tell him how that makes you feel. A woman who is loved by God is unstoppable!

_____

_____

_____

_____

_____

---

[26] P. Scazzero, *Emotionally Healthy Spirituality* (Grand Rapids, MI: Zondervan, 2017).
[27] B. & K. Gaultiere, *Journey of the Soul* (Grand Rapids, MI: Revell, 2021).

CHAPTER 3

Fear into Faith

After graduating from the crash course in maritime training, I landed on my first assignment in St. Vincent. Getting to the ship left me with trauma (my self-diagnosis). When I landed, I was picked up by a local cab driver, who the Miami-based tall ship company had hired to take me to the ship. I stepped into the vehicle, clutching my passport as tightly as I could; I was overcome with fear. As a young woman alone in an isolated place, I knew this situation wasn't safe.

As we pulled away from the airport and onto the winding roads of St. Vincent, I realized the driver was drunk. He let me know the ship had not yet docked and said he'd take me for a bite to eat, which resulted in several unplanned stops, one of which was his house. I locked myself in the bathroom there, praying in a panic for Jesus to save me. This was a terrible situation, and I turned my fear into faith that God would get me out of it. With all the courage I had left, I unlocked the door—I'd concluded there was no escape—and walked right back to the car and demanded he take me to the ship.

He did exactly what I told him to do and later made attempts to carry out his desire. I called aloud on the name of Jesus, which scared him. He angrily dropped me off at a dark, empty shipyard in the early morning hours. I panicked and began to cry hysterically as I searched for a place to hide. Then, a hostel caught my eye, but it was bolted shut with chains and locks. I beat on the door until my knuckles were bruised. Finally, an elderly security guard answered the door and let me in. He took pity on me and told me I could pay in the morning. He checked me into a room, where I immediately moved the dresser in front of the locked door in panic. Then I called my father and told him I needed to come home.

A woman back home, a family intercessor in our church, had called my parents hours before I did, letting them know they should intercede for my safety. She assured them I would call when I was safe. I fully expected my father would tell me to come home, but he did not. He had already flown to Trinidad to scare off a man who was following me home and he now said that I should stay the course and finish my commitment. He told me God was with me and was doing a work in me through all of this. As much as he wanted to rescue me again, he said that he could not. My heart sank as I hung up the phone, although now I know that call was the catalyst that shifted my dependence on my father as my rescuer to God, my Father. That phone call was a significant milestone in my life; my faith as God's daughter began to sprout wings. It came at one of the darkest moments of my young-adult life, yet it was a necessary one.

At some point, we must learn to press into God with our fears and allow him to turn them to faith. His love for us does that. Wise counsel and advice are critical, but everyone must learn to answer for their own yeses at some point. This was not how I imagined this adventure would start. I boarded my ship the next day and stayed on that ship for the next several weeks. I was still suffering from the trauma I had experienced. I had another nine months ahead of me with a ship full of male sailors. I later learned that the captain was also a "Jonah" type who was running from his own *yes*; he had insisted on figuring it out on his own, which led him to the sea.

Even in my imperfect, stubborn, strong-willed need to figure out my life plan on my own, God was at work in me. Finally, customers arrived; they had chartered the ship for a family birthday celebration for the week. I was still very guarded from my last experience. I regretted my decision to stay the course, but I was curiously intrigued by what God had planned for me on this adventure in the Caribbean.

One afternoon, we docked on a private island. As I was giving out cold beers from a cooler on the beach, one of the customers approached me and said, "Last night, I had a dream about you."

My guard went up immediately as I wondered why he was telling me this. He waved to his wife to join him and then said, "I dreamed of a beautiful clay pot that was intended for great purpose, but it had been marred in the process of life and sin. The beautiful vase was leaking water, which it was intended to hold. God wants to heal those broken places in your life."

I'd had no idea what this had to do with me—until it did!

He said, "You are that clay pot, and God is inviting you to allow him to put you back on his potter's wheel. He wants to restore you to your original purpose—to be full of water and to serve others from a place of wholeness and healing, which is your ultimate purpose."

> Yet you, Lord, are our Father. We are the clay, you are the potter, we are all the work of your hand. (Isaiah 64:8 NIV)

I thought it was a little weird, but I politely thanked him. That evening, I locked myself in my room and began to draw what he had spoken. I cried on my bedroom floor, asking God to make this sign clearer. The man also had mentioned that in three weeks' time, God would send another person to confirm this message was from him and to give me more direction. He also said I would be transferred to another ship.

I wrote down the date that was three weeks from then, and a lot happened during those three weeks. The next week, I was transferred unexpectedly from Grenada to the US & British Virgin Islands due to a resignation within the company. As with most activities mates and cruise directors, I was the center of the party. My primary responsibility was to ensure that customers had a great experience and to direct the activities for the week.

Three weeks to the date that the man had spoken to me, a quiet older gentleman, who had not really engaged during the entire week of cruise activities, approached me at the checkout desk. He said, "Young lady, God has a great plan for your life, and this is not it. Your sole mission in life is not to help people have fun but to help them find the truth of God's love. You will not fulfill your purpose on this ship."

I didn't want to hear what he had to say, but I knew he was speaking the truth from a place of love and humility. On that same cruise, a couple had asked if they could pray for me. Even in my shortcomings and directionless wandering, I knew that God was inviting me on a lifetime journey of following his lead, wherever that path led. Although I wanted an adventure, I also wanted the exact map to get there. I wanted to see the whole staircase, not just the next step. I wish I could tell you that two prophecies from complete strangers woke me up and that I surrendered all, but that was not the case. It definitely got my attention, but I was still determined to figure this out on my own. Some call it stubbornness, which might come from my Irish roots, and others call it the raw material for leadership. In my case, I think it was both.

I knew that God had a plan for me and that he was taking me up on the agreement. To be honest, I was still afraid of letting go and truly trusting God to lead me. I wanted the entire plan! While I was now aware he was guiding me, I impatiently continued to take actions into my own hands. I was battling the same question that Eve had battled in the garden. *Is God holding out on me?* I wondered. *Will he really lead me to fulfill my purpose? Can I really trust him fully?* From that place, the battle to control the outcome of my life continued. I suspect it is the same battle you quietly face as a woman too.

One of the most helpful strategies against our enemy, the devil, is to know his game. Where there is fear, we are a step closer to walking by faith and experiencing a miracle, if we recognize it. The enemy wants nothing more than for you to believe a lie that causes fear. Shame and fear give birth to control.[28] We must decide to partner with faith over fear, but it will require us to do some soul-searching. We first have to get to the root of the lie that causes shame and fear. Fear is often faith in reverse. When the enemy wants to cause confusion or sew doubt into our hearts about God's character, as he did with Eve, fear is a good indicator that he is at work. Here's the good news: we know this now. We know that Jesus made a way for us to overcome the schemes of the enemy, redeeming the sin of Adam and Eve through Jesus. We know when the enemy shows his cards of fear, we have the same power living in us that raised Christ from the dead, and it will overcome him with faith in who God says we are, with his authority!

---

[28] C. & B. Kylstra, *Restoring the Foundations: An Integrated Approach to the Healing Ministry* (Mount Juliet, TN: Restoring the Foundations International, 2000).

> Finally, be strong in the Lord and in his mighty power. Put on the full armor of God, so that you can take your stand against the devil's schemes. (Ephesians 6:10–11 NIV)

Choose to acknowledge that fear exists, and use it for your good. Choose to move in the direction of that fear, and turn it into a faith that propels you forward, trusting that God directs your steps. I was a horseback rider as a child; I have learned how to throw a bridle on fear and harness the power of Ephesians 6:10–11 to move toward radical trust and faith in God because of his love for me. And you can too!

Make It Personal

Have you ever experienced fear to such a degree that it caused you to take matters into your own hands or doubt God? Is there an area of your life where fear has been "eating your lunch"? What might be on the other side of that fear? What would it look like for you to add faith and trust in God to that particular situation? Is there a lie that you are believing about the thing you fear? Take a moment to write those down. Are they true? If not, simply break your agreement with that lie, and ask God what the truth is. Hearing from God for your journey ahead is a critical step in moving forward. Learning the discipline of identifying lies and replacing them with truth is a lifelong journey. You must get good at this in order to walk in the fullness that Christ has for you. Choose to bridle any fear you may have and move in faith! Take a radical step or decision today.

_____

_____

_____

_____

_____

CHAPTER 4

Not Every Opportunity Is a God Door

Several weeks passed, and a CEO of an Australian magazine company boarded my ship for a vacation. I had a pipe dream about writing and combining it with traveling the world, so I decided to slip a sample of my writing under her cabin door. I'd write about my travel adventures and exploration in the Caribbean and ask for her feedback. Now, I had no idea what kind of magazine she ran, but I saw an opportunity for writing, so I pursued it.

One day, while I was giving out beers on the beach again, she approached me. She said nothing about the writing sample but invited me to join her magazine company when I completed my contract on the ship; she wanted me to plan events for her company, which would also include some writing. I hadn't even prayed about this opportunity, but I knew it must be from God. I didn't bother to do my research and didn't even know what kind of writing it was until I arrived.

I had a thirty-day temporary travel visa, as we were both testing out my fit for the job before she sponsored me on a work visa. What happened in the next thirty days changed the course of my life. I learned a valuable lesson, the truth about God's love, and the importance of our promises to him.

Upon arrival, I thought I was living the dream! This office, with a balcony overlooking the city, was in one of Sydney's "happening" suburbs of young professionals. I slowly learned that the content of the magazine was cosmetic makeup and surgery, about which I could not have cared less. While I loved planning events, I longed for a mentorship in writing. I quickly realized that this job was not for me. This door of opportunity had looked so good, and the strong boss lady who ran her own company appeared to have everything the world deems successful. While I was not walking in my faith with full integrity at the time, the Lord continued to pursue my heart. I had given him my yes with my lips, but I had not surrendered every area of my life yet. He wanted my whole yes, meaning my soul, spirit, and body. He wanted my yes holistically.

I soon realized this was not going to be my long-term assignment, and I searched for answers yet again. This led me to travel across town to a well-known church in Australia that I'd vaguely heard about when I was in America. I sat in a crowd of hundreds of young people like me. I felt broken, defeated, and lost on what to do next. After an incredible worship experience, the pastor spoke in the service about a young woman who sounded a lot like me. Before my brain even processed what the rest of my body was doing, I found myself at the altar that night, sobbing on my knees. I simply wanted direction for the rest of my life and to find my place in the planet, contributing in the way that only I could. I realized, in all my searching, that I couldn't outrun God's love or the weight of my first yes. I realized at the altar that night that I was not meant to figure this out on my own. God was not a distant religious figure, from whom we take our marching orders like soldiers. He wasn't distant, and he didn't expect me to figure out my life alone; he also didn't expect me to figure out the God-ordained purposes he had in mind while I was in my mother's womb.[29]

I was designed for intimate communion with him, and through a relationship and trust, I would learn the process of a continual yes as I took steps along the journey. I was looking for identity and significance in a job and career and my accomplishments. I was looking for validation of the world's definition and measures of success. I had unknowingly put Jesus in the back seat to come along with me for the ride, rather than letting him take the wheel or, at minimum, sit with me in the front seat as my copilot.

Perhaps tears are forming in your eyes because you, too, have experienced this type of approach and have chased opportunities that

---

[29] Psalm 139:13.

were not God's doors for your life. Here is the good news: he never stops pursuing us because of his relentless love for humanity. He will chase you from the USA to the Caribbean to Australia, if he needs to. You have not messed up too big, and you can't run too far. He is serious about his commitments to pursue his children.

I left the service that night with a CD that spoke of God's purpose for my life. When I got back to my hotel room, I got into the shower and got on my knees. What happened next was incredible—I had never felt anything like I experienced that night, alone in my hotel room. I can only describe it as a hand on my back, holding me, as I wept for over an hour in repentance for my pride and rebellion. I cried and received peace and God's presence like I'd never experienced it in my life. I stayed there until my hands were pruned from the water, and I got up as a different person. I'd had a personal encounter with God himself, and he reminded me of my promise.

That week, I boarded a plane to Bali with the team from the magazine company for an annual planning retreat. I still can't believe the boss allowed me to go with them! I had only dreamed of experiencing the Indian Ocean and Bali. I was the resident event planner and was in charge of organizing fun activities for the team to explore Bali, which included adventure bike rides through the countryside, exercise classes, and surf lessons for the team. I couldn't believe this was my job. God began to stir my heart; I would take my journal to the hammock overlooking the Indian Ocean, and he began to speak. I knew he was calling me home, but I did not want to go. Going home without a real direction for my career made me feel like a failure. I encountered God but felt I had nothing to show for myself.

I typed an email to my parents, explaining why I had decided to come home. I had about seven days left on my return ticket and visa so I decided to spend that time in travel, in case I didn't make it back to Australia. I took a solo backpacking trip to Cairns, where I hiked and stayed in an incredible rain forest hostel on the coast. I ended my trip on Fitzroy Island, where one conversation with God changed my life. I took out my CD player as I watched sharks and jellyfish play on the water's edge, and I heard God's voice more clearly than ever before.

The woman speaking on the CD asked a simple question in her

sisterhood message: "Who are you?" I began to weep because I couldn't answer that question. I thought that I was defined by what I chose to do with my life. Now, I would argue that who you are *does* inform the work of your hands eventually, but it does not define who you are.

We are daughters of the most high God and he deeply loves us. He has a purpose and plans for our lives, and if we are brave enough to follow his lead, we will experience everything he intended in his time and his way. I can almost guarantee, however, that it will look nothing like you expected it would.

I didn't know who I was, aside from my external activity, striving for significance. I made God a promise that day; "God, I don't know who I am, but I will dedicate the rest of my life to allowing you to teach me who I really am." By the grace of God and lots of repentance along the way, I'm still walking out that promise. He is still teaching me, day by day, as my seasons in womanhood have significantly changed.

I do not know if we ever reach a finish line on this side of heaven. This is a relationship with the Creator of the universe, our Maker, who has ordained our days and counted the number of hairs on our heads. As long as you are breathing, he has a plan and purpose for you, right where you are. You don't have to travel halfway around the world to find him. He wants to meet with you right here, right now. He's never left you or forsaken you. He formed you in your mother's womb. No matter your story, He had you in mind! He thought the world would not be complete without you and the unique God-given gifts and talents you will contribute to cultivate a little heaven on earth.

We are all a part of one big story, and we are all connected by our Father in heaven. There is enough room for all of us to walk out God's callings and gifts on each of our lives. When all of our titles, accomplishments, and roles are stripped away, we are daughters and sisters with the same Father. I pray that wherever you are, these words jump off the page and into your heart. What you do does not define you. God defines you. While your purpose is to glorify him with the unique talents and gifts he has given you, your assignments will change—a lot. Don't get attached to or unknowingly defined by your assignment; it assuredly will change, perhaps by your own choice or by constraints forced upon you. Make the choice today that you will not be shaken by assignment changes but that you will allow God to teach you who you are and how to view your God-given assignments in each season.

Make It Personal

Are there any doors in your life that you need to yield to God? What doors are you praying for or beating down for yourself that has led you to striving? Take a moment to give over those areas to God, and ask Jesus to forgive you for trying to open those doors on your own. Ask God to open the right doors at the right time. Choose to be faithful, right where you are, until he urges you to take the next step.

_____

_____

_____

_____

Take a moment to pray and simply talk to God.

CHAPTER 5

Yielding to His Lead

"God, I surrender my life to wherever you lead. Please shut the doors that are not for me, and make the next step clear for me."

I am confident that you are a woman who desires to follow God's lead. For me, the assignments that followed after I returned to the United States were anything but glamorous, but they were priceless. My obedience in returning home required a surrender of my need to figure it out; it required clothing myself with great humility, against my will of being fiercely independent of anyone's help.[30] While I desperately longed for independence and autonomy, I simply did not have the finances to live on my own after my Caribbean and Australian travels. I moved home with my parents again and asked God to put me on the adult path to real purpose. At twenty-three and with a business degree in hand, I was nowhere closer to the vocational silver bullet I had idealized in my head than I had been previously, but I was growing in my intimacy with God and in my character.

I have learned that surrendering to follow Christ is not a one-time decision but a daily decision to follow, even when it doesn't make sense to us. God eventually opened doors for me as an executive assistant to the director of a Bible college in my hometown. Still, if I hadn't been living with my parents, I definitely would have barely made rent or been able to keep food in my pantry on my salary at the time. I often reflected on

---

[30] T. Baron, *The Cross and the Towel* (Tucson, AZ: Wheatmark, 2011), 11.

my agreement in Bali to return home and to follow God's lead. As I sat behind a desk under fluorescent lights, filing student grades, I thought I'd made a terrible mistake. For my wiring and personality, this attention to detail drained me most days, but what God was doing in me through this particular assignment was invaluable. He was transforming me from the inside as I chose to surrender daily, praying, "Thy will be done, not mine."

I began to recognize God's voice, and it became my lifeline to the adventure I longed to live in my heart. Practically, it looked like submitting to my boss's list of tasks each day while I felt I was simply dying inside. There were moments when God gave me glimpses of his goodness, and one of those moments was being sent to Ghana on behalf of my supervisor to audit a Bible college. It is easy to follow God when you experience what you pictured, but the road to those glorious moments looks vastly different than you could have imagined. We might wish for a straight shot to destiny, but I have found that moments of destiny come by the way of roads we would not choose for ourselves and are just that—moments.

When we give God our yes, we don't get to control how he chooses to prepare us or to get us where he wants us. In fact, I now understand it is impossible to be truly content with the journey God has marked out for us until we let go of what *we* had in mind.[31] I wonder how different my journey might have looked if I'd understood that destiny has moments that take a while to step into; it's not a race. In fact, I would pray that I could find the convergence of my passions, skills, and wiring quickly so I could get on with what I was supposed to do with my life, as if it were a race to a destination, and who I was when I arrived was a by-product. I now know it is the other way around. If we resist the work of yielding to God's process, we bypass the inner workings of character and the healing of our wounded hearts on our way to convergence.

Our yes to God is a yes to his routes, detours, and processes for becoming who we need to be so that whatever we put our hands to is an overflow of who we are. It takes time to unpack all the gifts that God has put inside of us, to refine the rough places of our personalities, and to discover freedom through unpacking our yesterdays. I did not realize that if we try to circumvent the long way around, those gifts often will be

---

[31] T. D. Jakes, "Let It Go," March 12, 2021, https://www.youtube.com/watch?v=DtOMWmY-stw.

untapped. We should walk the road less traveled, which is often filled with experiences, assignments, and seasons we do not care for and did not ask for. Having grown up in the United States, I approached my vocational calling as something I could achieve along a linear path and as a ladder to be climbed so I could clearly monitor my progress. My cultural lenses were near-sighted and not yet adjusted to God's kingdom way.

The sooner we fully embrace that God's ways are not our ways, the better equipped we will be to walk out our commitments and follow where God leads.

> "For My thoughts are not your thoughts, Nor are your ways My ways," says the Lord. (Isaiah 55:8–9)

Over twenty years later, I can appreciate the unassuming and somewhat normal assignments that have prepared me for the moments I get to step into from time to time. God is love, and love requires choice. God will not force himself on us; rather, he will give us the choice to surrender and yield control. I was a strong-willed redhead from a long line of strong-willed women, so submitting to God's mission for my life took more humility than I had when I started this journey. True freedom always requires choice, and true love chooses to yield and submit to—to "get under"—the mission of God for our lives, even if that route looks very different than what we imagined.

As I sat at my desk, day after day, at the Bible college, I wrestled with the dreams God put in my heart. Sometimes, I cried all the way from my parents' house to work. Some days, I reminded myself of the promise I made to God on Fitzroy Island; I promised I would follow his lead. I knew he had led me to this job, but I didn't know that an assignment from this job would be a catalyst for better understanding of my true calling. I learned how to hear God's voice while sitting in that small office, tolerating the fluorescent lights as I began to see "the light." God began to stir my heart for the students I processed at the international Bible colleges we supported. He stirred my heart for studying while I worked there too. I had access to professors who taught me how to do Greek and Hebrew word studies and to study the context of scripture, from which I still benefit today.

One day, a student from Africa walked into my office and sat down. He stared at a knick-knack on my desk; it was from my father and had the word *Dream* on it. He asked me why I had stopped dreaming. Then he said, "You will be asked to go to Africa in the next couple weeks, and you are to go without hesitation." He infused hope in my heart, even though I thought he was wrong, as I had just processed my boss's ticket to go to Ghana to check on one of the Bible colleges we started there.

A week went by as I pondered what this man had said to me. Then my boss walked into my office and told me that she couldn't go to Ghana. "Change my ticket to your name," she said, "I'd like you to go on my behalf."

I was floored by the opportunity. In a year's time, I had gone from a portable desk in the open air on the deck of a tall ship in the Caribbean to this small office cube, where it felt like my wings had been clipped. As I would sit there filing grades, I'd dream of meeting these students in person. Now, finally, I was going.

When I landed in Ghana and arrived at the Bible college, I could sense the disappointment of the director of the college, which he later made very clear, that the school had sent me instead of my boss. He said that I should not expect to speak because I was a woman—and an executive assistant at that. His mother, on the other hand, took me under her wing as a daughter and kept tabs on my whereabouts. She looked at me as if there was something different about me, and she believed I was carrying something they needed to hear. I was happy to simply do my job and participate. I knew there was something else I was to do there, but I was unsure of what. Meanwhile, I felt the Lord stirring and speaking to me about preparing an encouraging message to share with the students, which was in direct opposition to what the director told me. I kept reminding God of what the man had told me, and I thought he might be wrong. As I respectfully submitted to what was asked of me, I held on to the prompting I felt in my spirit from God.

As I sat in a chapel worship service, I saw a vision of Ezekiel like dead bones[32] walking and clanging around, making a notable sound. I peered out the window and saw what appeared to be fiery arrows shooting out from the school. When they hit the ground, the dead bones came back to

---

[32] Ezekiel 37:1–10.

life and walked toward the building. As they came into focus, I saw they were students coming to the building. As I wrestled with what I'd seen, it seemed like time stood still. I began to sweat, and then the director's mother leaned over to me and whispered, "What did you see?" She then leaned over to her son and told him that I needed to share what I'd seen.

I was in complete disbelief and utter shock that this was happening! The same man who had told me I could not speak to the students called me up to stand alongside him and share what I'd seen. I timidly walked up to the pulpit. As I began to share, the students broke out into weeping, shouting, and dancing. I didn't know what was going on. Then the director of the school told me, in front of the crowded sanctuary, that this had been their prayer as a school for some time. Their mascot and school symbol was a fiery arrow, which I had not known. Their mission was that students would go out like fiery arrows wherever they were sent, and find true life at the school.

Wow! I was in shock, and something awoke in my spirit that day. Perhaps I could trust God's Word in the midst of circumstances that often looked opposite of what I heard. Maybe I could submit to God's very interesting plan to get me where he wanted me to be. The next day, I was asked to go on a preaching tour to prisons and churches in the surrounding cities for the remainder of my visit. The director told me I should be ready to preach a word of encouragement to the people at each of those visits. In that season, I was learning to trust God's Word in my life and follow his lead, submitting to his ways on his terms.

Meanwhile, I was also reminded of my young-adult pastor back home, who had called on me to preach on a missionary journey to the Caribbean just months before. I was one of two female young adults on that trip, and he chose me to preach. It was as if God was catapulting me into a call I didn't know I had. If I was going to live the life of a true disciple and have the adventure I longed for, I had to learn to submit to God's ways and trust his Word in my life, regardless of the circumstances or what others might say.

Submission can have a negative connotation. As a mother of three, my strong-willed children have taught me that we are hardwired for insisting our own ways. It takes maturity to willingly yield and get under the mission of God and to yield to others. God knows best how to get us from where we are to where he wants us. How well we enjoy the journey is entirely up to us. In my experience, the pain and duration of the journey is prolonged by resisting. We wear ourselves out, trying to go our own way, or worse, we waste priceless moments being frustrated and angry, and we miss the beauty of the season we are in. Many times, my kids are insistent on doing something their own way. I just sit there and let them wear themselves out, and then they are willing to listen. As a mother, I have to choose the moments to step back; I have to assess the risk of letting them figure it out the hard way.

My son was once so angry that he'd lost screen time, which happened often, that I sent him to his room for a short time to cool off. I have learned there is no sense in trying to have a rational conversation with a five-year-old until he has calmed down. Twenty minutes of tantrum ended up with a tired little boy, lying on my lap, eventually calm enough to tell me what was bothering him at school that day. I have been like my son with God in seasons that have been very difficult for me and have used my strength in the wrong way. As a mother, I often think, I wish they would just yield to my direction and save all that energy for something good. I am certain God has had to stand aside, just as I have as a parent, and let me wear myself out a couple times in my life journey thus far. Eventually, I find myself humbled, worn out, and asking for his help.

Yielding does not mean weakness. Somewhere along the journey as a woman, a lie is sewn into our hearts that yielding is a sign of weakness, but it is the opposite. When I was a young adult, fresh out of college, I saw marriage as an act of weakness because it meant yielding my life plan to someone else's. That is difficult to acknowledge, but it is the truth! I have since learned that it is actually quite the opposite and that the walls of self-protection and a fortress of independence would need to come down if I was going to live in a healthy relationship with God and others. I can see why the enemy of our souls, Satan, would want to sew one of the most dangerous lies into our hearts at very formable stages in our lives as women. If we believe that yielding to God or anyone else is a sign of weakness because we see nothing but pain and suffering, then we will avoid the most important decisions of our lives that require a yielding, not only to God's purpose for our lives but the great calling of family and motherhood as well. There is real confusion about the word *weakness* defined as "lack of power, influence or strength of character."³³ The truth is that until we can embrace our weakness, God cannot fully show himself strong in our lives. It is not until we yield that we can boast all the more in our weakness and learn what real grace means on a personal level.

> "My grace is all you need. My power works best in weakness." So now I am glad to boast about my weaknesses, so that the power of Christ can work through me. (2 Corinthians 12:9)

I don't know about you, but I don't like to be weak or admit weakness. Who does? The key to true strength is only unlocked in our lives when we realize that God's kingdom seems upside down to the one where we now live. True strength is found only when we boast in our weakness and God's power, so that all will know that God is real, and he chooses to shine through us as a beacon of hope to the world around us. In our ability to choose meekness, bringing our God-given power and strength under control and choosing to yield to God and his way of doing things, we tap into the secret of God's kingdom and his strength. The enemy sells us lies and seeds of doubt that God might be holding out on us, as he did to Eve in the garden.³⁴ The real truth is actually found in our submission to God's mission and complete surrender to embrace our weaknesses. The real opportunity is found on the other side of submission for God to shine through us, as he leads us into our God-given vocational assignments in life. Embracing our weaknesses should not be misinterpreted as thinking less of ourselves; it simply means we have a proper view of who God is and our identity as his daughters. This posture gives us a healthy self-esteem and a proper view of ourselves to branch out and serve others in our God-given gifts and talents while carrying his heart.

> Charm is deceptive, and beauty is fleeting; but a woman who fears the LORD is to be praised. (Proverbs 31:30)

---

[33] "Weakness," *Oxford Learner's Dictionaries*, Oxford University Press (2022), https://www.oxfordlearnersdictionaries.com/us/definition/english/weakness.
[34] Genesis 2–3.

Make It Personal

Are there any areas in which you know you've been resisting God's lead in your life? Are there any areas of your life in which you have a hard time submitting your will or trusting God's Word in your life? Take a moment to acknowledge them and write them down. Then, simply repent and ask God to take the lead in that particular area. Remember that submission is simply getting under the mission of God for your life. It brings protection and security. It requires hearing God's voice and doing what he says, with his help.[35] I know God is speaking, and you can hear him.

_____

_____

_____

---

[35] M. Batterson, *How to Hear the Voice of God* (Colorado Springs, CO: Multnomah, 2017), 19.

CHAPTER 6

Confronting Competition and Comparison

I grew up an only child 50 percent of the time; the other 50 percent of the time I was either bossing or pushing my sweet little sister around. If we only knew as children what we know as adults, we'd all likely make different choices. It has taken a long time to learn how to manage the blind spots in my strong personality and strength. While there are a lot of upsides to being fiercely independent and an entrepreneurial driver of initiatives, these very traits also have dangerous blind spots. While God does uniquely design us with our various personalities, he also asks us to submit to his ways and to one another out of reverence for him, whether those come easily or not. I now realize that we are hardwired for greatness because we are made in the image of our God, who is great. That said, greatness in God's eyes often feels opposite to how the world defines it. We are hardwired for attention, significance, and belonging. It is only later in life that we discover that only God can truly fill our needs for significance and belonging. We learn as adults to perform well in life for love and attention, as the way of culture. If we don't realize that we don't have to compete for God's approval, we will run ourselves ragged trying to earn approval that we already have in God, or worse, we will compete with everyone.

God's arms are big enough for all of us and our uniqueness. We can let go of competing for attention and validation or a place of significance.

The place of significance was settled when Jesus died for us. His great sacrifice settled our value once and for all, regardless of who did or did not validate our value along the way. When we realize that no one on the earth has exactly the same DNA or wiring to see the world the way we see it, we will understand there is no one with whom to compete—God makes designer originals with his signature on each of us. You can no longer copy or compete with others because God broke the mold when he created you. We share his image as our Father, but no one can take our places in the world. Jobs, positions, and titles can certainly be shared, but no one will fill them quite like you will. Sure, others can take the title, but they are not you!

We must rest assured that there is no need to compete with anyone else for significance, attention, or value. The only one who matters has already settled that we are significant to his plan for humanity, and we can call for his attention in any place at any time. In fact, he is waiting in anticipation that we will give him our affection. After all, that is why he sent his Son, Jesus, to bridge the great sin chasm, to reconcile God and humankind to live in intimate relationship for eternity, starting right here on earth.

> But God demonstrates his own love for us in this: While we were still sinners, Christ died for us. (Romans 5:8)

I made the varsity basketball team as a freshman in high school—and I was the best bench-warmer all year. I was excited if I got the last two minutes of playing time in the fourth quarter. I didn't have the same level of skills that others had, but I had heart! I had grit and a tenacious attitude and fortitude that won me a spot on the team. I was invited to tryouts with the juniors and seniors, which required a three-mile run in under twenty-four minutes. I hated running and still don't enjoy it unless it has a direct purpose to what I'm trying to accomplish or playing a sport to distract me. My stepfather charted out my course so I could practice on the weekends on our long, country dirt road. One day, my sister wanted to run with me, and my raw, underdeveloped gift of entrepreneurship and competition got the best of me. As an immature girl, I pushed my little sister in the dirt. She had tears in her eyes as I reminded her there was only one athlete in the family. That was so ugly! As an adult, I look at that childish moment and realize that many of us still have not grown out of those childish ways. Rather than using our God-given gifts to help advocate for others and bring them along, we compete with one another for first place. Let's settle that right now; we all have first place in our Father's heart. We do not need to compete with one another for his attention or affection. We were all formed and fashioned with unique gifts and talents to share with others, not to compete with others. It requires great humility to submit our gifts to one another and yield to others going first when we'd rather be first. God's Word and promises to us are clear:

> For those who exalt themselves will be humbled, and those who humble themselves will be exalted. (Matthew 23:12 NIV)

Once my prefrontal cortex was fully developed, and I became a wife and eventually a mother, I began to reframe and refocus the "drive" that would compete and compare with others into asking God to help me become the best possible version of myself. I decided to become a champion for my sisters, my spouse, and my family. I decided to find the joy in seeing others fulfill their dreams and cross the finish line of life with God too! I learned that my promise to follow Jesus would look like cheering others along their paths as a way of living as a kingdom citizen. If we claim to love God but hate our brothers and sisters, we are lying to ourselves.[36] A life well lived cannot be lived alone. We were never created for that, which means a meaningful and successful life will include working with others toward a vision much bigger than ourselves, as we yield to one another along the way. The workplace certainly gives us opportunities to practice this concept, but I would say that these principles are even better learned in the context of family dynamics. In order to have healthy families, we have to stop seeing the world as a competition; rather, it's a great collaboration project. The mission is to become the best version of yourself for those you lead and love so they, too, can become the best version of themselves and contribute positively to the world around them. This sounds beautiful in theory, but these are the hard yards for which we need the Holy Spirit's

---

[36] 1 John 4:20.

help as we die daily to old thinking and put on the mind of Christ as we continue to walk out our most important yes.

> Who has known the mind of the Lord so as to instruct him? But we have the mind of Christ. (1 Corinthians 2:16 NIV)

When I finally said I do to my husband after graduate school, I wrestled with the art of complementing, not competing in, my marriage. My husband is an avid reader and researcher, and early in our marriage, I tried to compete with his reading list. I would get frustrated by how quickly he processed information and could thoroughly research something to make an informed opinion. Now, almost a decade later, I've learned to complement those strengths and lean into them, rather than compete with him. I am well-read now because I let my husband do most of the research in our family and church libraries. And he leans into my ability to get stuff done and move the vision ahead in collaboration with others. As we learn to yield our blind spots to God and use our strengths to complement rather than compete, we glorify God in whatever we do. I wondered how God would weave our lives together with our very different experiences, passions, and desires. I often remind myself of my *yes* to God in marriage. That yes to God has given me the strength, as a married woman, to yield to God's lead in marriage through my husband's lead at times. This would not have been possible if I hadn't learned how to yield to God as a single woman first.

There is no way to live God's way without renewing your mind with the Holy Spirit's help and walking out your yes each day. When I made the transition from looking outward in comparison to looking inward and acknowledging my blind spots, I began to see transformation as I submitted those areas to God for help. We must choose to be kind to ourselves in the process. In business or any industry, we are taught to benchmark to measure progress or see how we are doing, compared to what we think is the standard or best practice. There is truth in this concept, but the problem becomes when we benchmark our journeys and lives with the neighbors next door, our colleagues, and others around us. We make the mistake of comparing the entirety of our lives with what we see from a distance, and we unknowingly idolize someone else's success and mitigate our own progress. We must choose to discipline our eyes for God alone and allow him to define what our successful life looks like to him, not to others. As we learn to pace ourselves and submit our timelines and measuring sticks to the Lord, we learn to trust him with the outcomes he requires of us, not our sisters or brothers. Saying yes to God requires our allowing him to heal the deepest issues of our brokenness, layer by layer, until we resemble him more and more and live from his approval, not for it.

> For all have sinned and fall short of the glory of God, being justified as a gift by His grace through the redemption which is in Christ Jesus. (Romans 3:23–24)

Make It Personal

In which area of your life do you compare and compete with others? Do you think this is God's best for you? What kind of fruit does it produce in your life?

_____

_____

_____

Are there any lies you believe about yourself or others that cause you to compete and compare yourself to others?

_____

_____

_____

Take a moment to break agreement with any lies you discover, and ask God for the truth. Ask God if there is anyone who might have contributed to your believing those lies. If anyone comes to mind, forgive that person by name.[37] Every time you think about those lies, stop and replace them with the truth of what you heard God say about that area over and over! Pray, asking Father God to help you believe the truth (e.g., "Father, forgive me for believing that lie.").

_____

_____

_____

---

[37] K. & M. Luse, *Connect Up Healing Prayer Ministry Training Manual* (Harrisonburg, PA: Connect Up Ministry, 2018).

CHAPTER 7

Unpacking Your Yesterdays

As women, we all have a unique story. After the birth of my first child, Hanna, I wrestled with my identity in ways that had always been there but were starting to resurface. I remember taking my first solo road trip to my father's beach condo with Hanna. I was searching for answers on what it meant to balance my roles as a woman in life and was internally struggling. I was filled with myriad emotions in having a daughter, but I didn't have words for what I was feeling at the time. I began to realize how many competing lies I needed to weed out of my heart and my mind about what it meant to be a Christian woman, a successful woman, a mother, and a wife, all of which I desired to become. I realized how much renewing my mind needed, and I asked myself where I had come to my conclusions about what it meant to be a successful woman with many roles.

I had found my rhythm as a single woman and had even grasped a rhythm of living as a married woman in my own skin for a couple years. It was not until my eldest daughter came along that something inside of me awoke, and I also realized my own brokenness at a new level. I knew that I had to begin this journey of returning to my family of origin[38] and unpacking the lies I'd picked up along life's journey about womanhood. Then I could equip Hanna with the tools she would need as a woman one day. I also knew that it was impossible to teach and train anyone if you don't walk it out yourself first, as a matter of integrity. I did not want Hanna to struggle with her identity as a strong Christian female or struggle

---

[38] P. Scazzaro, *Emotionally Healthy Spirituality* (Grand Rapids, MI: Zondervan, 2017).

with her why-am-I-here, like I did. I wanted her to fully embrace herself, her strength, and her femininity, in alignment with God's truest design for her life. This desire for her to walk in greater freedom was the catalyst that unlocked greater levels of freedom in my journey.

It is funny how sometimes we won't do something for ourselves, but for our children, we will scale mountains. I remember an incident on the playground at Hanna's first soccer season. A big boy pinned my then-five-year-old daughter on the playground and kicked her with his cleats. I was eight months pregnant with our son and scaled a rock wall to throw this child off my daughter. Yes, I threw him! In that moment, I didn't debate whether that was a good idea; my love for my daughter compelled me to do something I would never otherwise do in my own strength or deliberation. Sometimes, the deeper journey of freedom and truth in our lives requires a catalyst of some kind, but whatever that is, take the invitation! It will change your life.

This weeding process took me years, and I still take regular inventory for any lies that I believe. I have to stop and ask myself, *Is this true?*[39] Does it align with God's Word? Is this what God says about me and this situation? Is there something I need to change about the way I'm looking at this? From whom can I learn? What resources can help me with changing my mind on this situation when I can't see clearly?

My husband and I decided to kill the grass in our yard one year because there were so many weeds; we would simply start over. To my surprise, after the beautiful fresh grass began to grow, those pesky weeds did too. The difference was that I was very aware of it because we had already weeded the entire yard. I was on guard against the weeds creeping up in our yard. The same is true for our hearts. It may take some intentional work to kill the myriad of lies beneath the surface of our lives, but then, we will be much more attuned to not allowing them to get out of hand and removing them when they first pop up so they don't spread!

The first lie I had to tackle was the idea that somehow all women are the same; I'd already disqualified myself a long time ago from being a godly mother and wife. I simply believed that I wasn't the mother-and-wife type of person, whatever that was. In fact, I thought that only a certain

---

[39] K. & M. Luse, *Connect Up Healing Prayer Ministry Training Manual* (Harrisburg, PA: Connect Up Ministry, 2018).

type of woman or personality could be married and "easily" submit to God's structure of the family design, calling men to lead their homes and loving their wives as Christ loved the church. I had a distorted view of what leading your home looked like. I disqualified myself out of the gate and finally walked down the aisle at twenty-eight years old, in complete faith that God would help me to become a wife. I struggled deeply with this decision because I had convinced myself that I did not have what it took to be a godly Christian wife. The first deeply rooted lie that I had to renounce was that I was not "marriage material." I had convinced myself of this lie because I did not like any of the domestic responsibilities that came with the role. I had issues with authority and enjoyed my freedom and independence, having been on my own for a while. I did not want to submit my plans or will to anyone else who would slow me down from what I had in mind. I had spent most of my life doing that under the cover of my parents and had tasted the freedom of adulthood, so why would I willingly submit myself to someone else? The deep-seated lies and ungodly beliefs were planted into my subconscious as a child of the 1980s. I've since learned that children from birth to mid-young adulthood are excellent observers but poor interpreters of situations and circumstances around then. I grew up in a broken home, which caused me to bounce back and forth between my mom's and dad's homes. As I grew up, being a poor interpreter of the situation, I subconsciously took on the shame that I somehow had responsibility in their breakup, and I never processed the pain until I was an adult. False responsibility started young for me, and I carried those heavy rocks in my backpack for most of my childhood until my young adult years, when I realized those rocks were getting too heavy to carry. They were impacting my present, and they had to go.

Those seeds were already planted by the enemy, who attempted to thwart God's plan for me and confuse me on my calling to a family of my own. If you have experienced something similar, you know that the fight against walking in your true identity starts young. John 10:10 tells us that the enemy comes to steal, kill, and destroy our lives. He is masterful at exploiting emotionally vulnerable moments in our lives and tempting us to lend our agreement to lies we believe because of the pain of dealing with those moments.

I wrestled deeply with God about whether marriage was the right next step for me. I remembered the conversation I'd had with God on the beaches of Fitzroy Island in Australia on one of my many single exploits. I remembered the agreement I made to follow Jesus wherever he led me. I asked if the next sunset I would watch could be with someone who loved him too; I was starting to feel lonely as I traveled alone. After my then-fiancé walked out on me during premarital counseling on the topic of children, I knew I had more digging to do. I sat in my room in my apartment, alone, journaling and using a tool called *listening prayer*.[40] I was mad and frustrated that we'd been asked to talk about having a family at that point in our journey. I had just mustered enough courage to consider marriage, and now, I had to discuss having a family too! I remember the Holy Spirit's comfort that day, and all I heard was that this was the husband I'd asked for. He didn't come in the package or story in which I thought he would come. He was more like "Domestic Danny" than well-traveled "International Ivan." (My husband came up with that analogy, not me.) We laugh about it now, but following Jesus and saying yes to him meant that we had to let go of what we had in mind in order to experience the fullness of this God adventure called life.

While I knew that marriage was my next step in my journey with Christ, I was fearful that I might have to lay down my preferences and who I really was. I won't lie; marriage will definitely refine and smooth out the rough edges of our various personalities, but in no way is God calling us to change the essence of how he made us. We might have drawn a box of what we think we have to be, rather than embracing who we are and redefining the role to fit us. God does call us to mature in our view of him and ourselves, which requires some boot-camp conditions, like marriage and children, that will require death to our own will at times. I have found, in the process of laying our preferences aside to follow Christ's lead, is that if it is truly from him for our lives, the dream will continue to resurrect within us. It may not look like what you had in mind, or it may not be on your timetable, but it will be resurrected.

After I fully submitted to God's will and followed through on my promise to allow him to lead me first, I asked my fiancé, Jeremy, if he would marry me—with a *maybe* to children. God was working on Jeremy's heart as a son, too, during this time. Jeremy said he would marry me, with

---

[40] L. Payne, *Listening Prayer* (Grand Rapids, MI: Baker Publishing Group, 1999), 19.

a maybe to children, knowing that I would follow Jesus wherever he led us. In that moment, I knew that my definition of a successful woman was off, and it was there that the remodeling and renovating of my definition of being a woman began.

What if the successful woman came in all kinds of personality packages and looked completely different than what I had in mind? This was a paradigm shift for me. It was not until my first year of marriage that I realized I had believed a lie—that only weak women got married. I was dead wrong! Strong women came in all kinds of different personality types and life paths. I've now been married for over a decade, and I know that submitting takes the kind of strength that only comes from God, to serve in all the roles he calls us to in womanhood, clothed in meekness and strength under control. The strength comes in submission to Father God and a willingness to lay our strengths, skills, talents, and desires at his feet and the humility to ask for guidance on how to manage the strength he has given us. After all, he does know us best and what he intended for our lives before our very conception.[41]

> For you created my inmost being; you knit me together in
> my mother's womb. (Psalm 139:13)

His handiwork marks each of us uniquely, and he has a unique design to display his glory through our lives. This takes time. I thought that I had to unwrap all the gifts God gave me as quickly as possible and figure out how they all worked together, as if this life was a race. I see this with my young children, who begin getting birthday gifts from family before their actual birthdays. They do not willingly choose to wait! They want to open all the gifts at one time in a hurry. This is a childlike approach to unpacking the beautiful gifts within us that are intended to be opened at different times and seasons to be enjoyed fully. This process cannot be rushed by our own desire; rather, we should entrust it to God's plan and process for our lives. This takes us back to the first yes. For some, yes means waiting a little longer for the right relationship, to step into your dream job or vocation, or to say yes to the dress. Whatever your next yes to God, he

---

[41] Psalm 139:13.

loves you and will never lead you into harm's way— but you must choose to follow his lead.

> Again I say to you, if two of you on earth do anything they ask, it will be done for them by my Father in heaven. And you ask in prayer, you will receive, you have faith. (Matthew 18:19–22 NIV)

Pray the following with me:

I will submit my passions, desires, talents, and skills to your plan, Father God. I ask you to lead me into the best use of those in every season of my life, even if it is not the plan I would have chosen for myself. I trust your leadership in my life and give you permission to reveal any lies that I believe about what it means to be a godly woman. Help me to have the courage to keep saying yes to this journey of discovery with you. Amen.

Make It Personal

Are there any lies you believe about yourself or what it means to be a woman?[42]

_____

_____

Finish the following sentence: I break agreement with the lie that

_____

_____

---

[42] K. & M. Luse, *Connect Up Healing Prayer Ministry Training Manual* (Harrisburg, PA: Connect Up Ministries, 2018), 63.

What is the truth, or what do you want to give me in exchange for that lie?

___

Ask yourself if what you hear aligns with God's Word? Does it align with God's character? Seek spiritual guidance or process with a pastor or trusted friend who is also walking out her faith journey.

___

___

CHAPTER 8

Letting Go of Control

When I graduated from undergraduate school, I put pressure on myself to figure out quickly what to do with my talents and gifts so I could make a living and survive on my own. I now know a better approach would have been to focus on learning to hear God's voice, trust his lead more than my own plan, and discover and understand who I was as a person with the gifts God gave me to create value in the world. After working as a recruiter in both nonprofit and education, I've concluded that very few people know exactly what and how they will contribute value to society without some experimentation and failure. The earlier we can accept God's design for us and submit to his path, which will require seasons in the valley of weakness, the less discouraged we will get along this narrow road.

I was the valedictorian of my senior class in a small country high school and an award-winner for Most Likely to Succeed. I look back and see God's hand on my life, even when I had the wrong idea of the path to success. I put incredible pressure on myself to live up to the speech I gave about finding the true road to success, the narrow one, and actually succeeding. My road has not looked "successful," according to the image and path I had in my mind. My pride has often gotten in the way of surrendering to the road less traveled, which is one of trust and following where God leads. The road to God's definition of success and living in God's kingdom is indeed a narrow one, in the sense that it often feels upside down from the wide road everyone else seems to be traveling with relative success, as the world defines it.

THE MOST IMPORTANT YES

Our most important yes should be followed by defining what success in God really looks like for us and an internal audit of all the mindsets on what a successful life should look like. That is terrifying for some and an adventure for others. I was somewhere in between, as one who desired an adventure but was riddled with fear and anxiety of the unknown, with a desire to do something meaningful with my life. I deeply longed to cling to the markers of worldly success but found a greater growing dissonance in my heart between what I thought I was supposed to do and what I felt God was calling me to do with my life.

As the stakes get higher and we choose to get married or have children, we unknowingly cling even tighter to the mile markers and security life rafts that society determines as a successful life. You know them too. There is nothing wrong with those things, but when they become the drivers that lead us into becoming workaholics or addicted to adrenaline and hustling, and it causes chronic emotional distress, we need to look under the surface of our thinking and realign our thoughts with God's on this matter. When others say strive and hustle, God may tell us to rest. When the world promotes control and unhealthy ownership of outcomes, we may need to let go, releasing control, and learn to genuinely trust God for the outcome. We often do not realize that we have a death grip on something until we are forced to let go by outside forces, such as job loss, illness, or circumstances out of our control, like a global pandemic. Rather than seeing these as the end of something that drives us into obsessive control, we can learn to lean into the change and embrace the new, which God is birthing in and through us.

The door to the shame of not meeting our own expectations leads to blame, fear, and feelings of failure and hopelessness. This either keeps us stuck or propels us into controlling behaviors that drive us to accomplish more and more. We get to choose whether we live a life of obsessive control, in fear of losing traction, or we learn to lean back into the loving arms of our Savior and follow his lead. Accomplishments are not bad until they become the fix you live for that slowly erodes your soul and meaningful relationships. The good news is that change can happen when we are fully awake, self-aware, and desire to change.

Today may be your catalyst to realize you've been living up to your expectations of success in an unhealthy way, as I've experienced. When I became aware of the shame, fear, and control cycles operating in my life, I was horrified. After the birth of our third child, I felt completely out of control. It happened to collide with some delayed postpartum depression and hindered my ability to fully function for about six months. I felt so much shame and fear because I couldn't function or perform, as much as I tried. Meanwhile, I continued to hear God whisper to me that I needed to rest for what was ahead. I had no choice but to trust his lead to rest at a time that didn't seem very restful, with a newborn, two toddlers, the launch of a church, and a merger and acquisition at work. I submitted myself to God's lead and took a forced rest for six months (as best I could, as a mother of three young children) and recovered. I battled shame, fear, and control with surrender, faith, and releasing the outcome to God. I reminded myself of God's promises to me during that difficult season and gave him my trust to lead me out of the darkness I felt there.

The first step into a life of freedom—a life apart from shame, fear, and control—is being aware that this cycle exists and is wreaking havoc on our lives.[43] It is often a result of driving ourselves to achieve a version of success to which we feel we must measure up. There is a better way, but it will take a commitment to rework how we think and to keep watch over our lives to ensure we don't fall into the trap of measuring up again. Second, Jesus made a way to reverse the curse of sin. We must repent and confess that we fell into these sin patterns and ask for help. We must decide to move towards the thing we fear and choose faith over fear. Fear needs our agreement to be empowered. It is like a three-headed dragon that gets larger and fiercer as we feed it the breakfast of performance, while we're riddled with shame, fear, and control. Without a host, the enemy has no power and cannot complete his agenda to wreak havoc in our lives.[44]

> The thief comes only to steal and kill and destroy; I have come that they may have life, and have it to the full. (John 10:10)

---

[43] C. & B. Kylstra, *Restoring the Foundations: An Integrated Approach to Healing and Freedom* (Mount Juliet, TN: Restoring the Foundations International, 2001).
[44] John 10:10.

Last, we have to choose surrender and trust, rather than entertain the temptation to control. Then we can experience the full life God promises us, living life by his standards for a successful and meaningful life. Take a few minutes before moving on to the next chapter to reflect and put this in action.

Make It Personal

What is your definition of success? Write it out. Does it align with God's definition for a successful life? Read Micah 6:8, and then write it out below:

_____

_____

Are you are currently struggling with shame, fear, and control in some areas of your life? Could areas of shame and fear be driving you to fulfill how you have envisioned success for yourself? This is the opportunity to reflect and be honest with yourself and God. Write them down and disempower their hold in your life.

_____

_____

Think through the opposite of these areas of shame, fear, and control that need to be reversed in your life.

Repent for this area in which you've felt shame. Give it to Jesus. Take a moment and ask what the truth is. Write that truth here.

_____

_____

What is the opposite of the very thing you fear? Take a moment to thank God for the opposite, and say it out loud. Lend your faith to it.

_____

_____

What is the opposite of the very thing you are trying to control? Take a moment to give it to God. Give it to the Lord, and tell him that you choose to trust him in this area. Ask for help in waiting. Is there anything you need to do in the waiting? Whatever it is, obey him. If you're not sure, share this with a trusted sister who also is living life from a Christ-centered perspective.

_____

_____

CHAPTER 9

Weeding the Garden

It is quite possible to say yes to Jesus with all of your heart and still have a lifetime of weeding the garden of your heart and mind. Your yes actually means accepting a lifelong process of God's sanctification work so you can reflect him more fully.

First, you must know and understand that God's ways are not your ways. Most likely, you will need to change your thinking if you are going to walk with Christ. The thoughts are just the fruit of the beliefs in our hearts. The true roots originate in the garden of the heart.[45] As you change your mind and align your thoughts with his, it will feel a lot like weakness. Your weakness is often God's opportunity to put his glory on display in your life, as you trust his ways over your own.[46]

> For my thoughts are not your thoughts, neither are your ways my ways, declares the Lord. As the heavens are higher than the earth, so are my thoughts higher than your thoughts. (Isaiah 55:8–9)

Accepting this truth postures our hearts in submission to God's mission for our lives. When I said yes to Jesus, I came face-to-face with my issues around—submission. I made some strong agreements in my heart and mind along they way. I thought submission was for the weak,

---

[45] A. Philips, The Garden Within (Nashville, TN: Nelson Books, 2023), 4-5.
[46] M. Batterson, *Do It for a Day* (New York City, NY: The Crown Publishing Group, 2021), 3.

and I could not identify with that. Since making those ungodly agreements in my mind, I have learned that it is actually in my weakness that Christ can be made strong.

Courage and strength are found in our ability to get under the mission of God for our lives and to follow his lead. We will not experience the true power of Christ living in us until we are willing to give God access to the weak areas of our lives. It is a journey, and God is more patient with us than we are with ourselves most of the time.

I have since changed my mind about the power of submission. Meekness is defined as power under control. True submission is a willingness to get under the mission of God for your life and obey God at his Word, regardless of how you may feel about it. Submitting to God's plan for your life might lead to the bonds of marriage and children. It might require relinquishing control of that area by trusting God's timing for the family you've dreamed of when it hasn't happened yet. For others, it might be remaining single or saying, "I do." Whatever the reason, I did not see myself as a mother of multiple children. As I've mentioned, when Jeremy and I went through a premarital course at my church, he left the session when I could not give a clear answer on building a family. I hadn't given it much thought before that point, but I had picked up some lies along my journey; I believed that I was not the "mother" type. I had disqualified myself, although God clearly had not. I had to untangle the web of ungodly beliefs and lies that I associated with being a married woman and a mother so that God could equip me for my job in the calling of family.

The enemy of our souls, Satan, is ruthless and desires to sell us lies when we are very young, distorting situations and circumstances to thwart the plans God has for us. My parents were divorced when I was an infant, and I believe the enemy wanted nothing more than to sow a seed of fear that I, too, did not have what it takes to stay in a marriage and raise a family. He, however, did not have the last word; thankfully, I caught on to his agenda early enough to uproot some of the fear, shame, and control that held those lies in place.

We all have places in our lives where the enemy has attempted to thwart the callings and plans that God has for us, but if we resist him and seek the truth, God's Word will prevail. We must choose to hold on to

God's truth about our future and reject every lie and pretension that works against the truth in our lives.[47]

> Submit yourselves, then, to God. Resist the devil, and he will flee from you. (James 4:6)

Discovering and holding on to God's truth and choosing to align your life with God's truth about you may take you on a different path than you saw for yourself. This is evidence of the transformation of a life submitted to Christ. Submission is not a women's issue; it is a leadership issue. All healthy leaders are submitted under someone else's authority. In fact, Jesus praised the centurion who asked for his servant to be healed. When Jesus went to the centurion's house to heal his servant, the man responded with,

> But just say the word, and my servant will be healed. For I myself am a man under authority, with soldiers under me.[48]

In other words, I understand the authority of God and submit myself to God's order of things, and I willingly submit myself to your Word. Wow! How incredible is this man's faith—and so it is with us, as women. God made no mistake by creating us as women for such a time as this. His divine design reveals destiny. As women, we willingly choose to submit our will under the mission of God, regardless of what it costs us. We are transformed in the process as we grow in meekness, power under control. Getting under the mission of God requires a posture of humility and strength to lay down our pride, plans, hopes, and desires. We do this in exchange for a divine relationship, built on trusting that God knows the deepest desires of our hearts and the best paths to take us there. The root cause that keeps us from submitting to God's order and his will for our lives is fear and pride. It is the original sin that Eve faced in the garden of Eden when she entertained the enemy's lies about God holding out on her for giving her limits. Ouch!

For a moment, Eve allowed the seed of doubt to be planted in her heart

---

[47] 2 Corinthians 10:5.
[48] Matthew 8:8–9.

which gave birth to taking a bite of the forbidden fruit that she was told not to eat. Rather than submitting to God's will for her life and his limits, it cost her much more than she was willing to pay. We are her daughters and like her, we also can be tempted by this same lie of fear, that God is somehow holding out on us. We can be tempted to avoid submitting to God's leading and promptings because of our own pride, which prevents our fully trusting God's ability to make us into everything he called us to be!

It is critical to your spiritual formation to know that your yes will require thousands of yeses to submit and yield to Christ's leading in your life at every new chapter. It will require laying down your pride and self-sufficiency and clothing yourself in humility. You must trust and believe that, just as Jesus's submitting to the Father's will to die for us brought eternal life for all of us, your submission is not just about you. Your submission is about so many others whom you will influence as a mother, daughter, friend, sister, and leader in the area God has called you to influence, directly or indirectly.

I remember planting a few flowers in my little patio garden in my first townhome. I am not a gardener, nor do I enjoy it at all, but I did want some flowers in my patio. As a complete amateur, I pulled the weeds from the flower bed and was disgusted to find out that within two weeks, those rascals were back again. It was so discouraging. I didn't know the additional measures I needed to take to ensure that the weeds' roots were gone. I failed to get the root of the weed and learned that these weed seeds were carried through the air from other plants and landed right back into my flower bed. As I studied how to get rid of the weeds in my new garden area, I found so many parallels about the lies that grow in the gardens of our hearts and minds. I realized that, so many times, I have only uprooted part of the lie in my mind without getting to the root in my heart. Until I followed that weed to the seed deeply planted in the garden of my heart and mind, I would continue to be overgrown with weeds, and the beautiful flowers often got choked out!

A lie can be as simple as, "I will never let a man tell me what to do." This weed is not the real seed. The root of the seed that has to be dug out is likely deep under the soil, in a memory from somewhere that included a situation in your past where you made an agreement due to pain you experienced. I had to give myself permission to go there first and understand where I came into agreement with that lie. That lie was attached to a deep seed of hurt and pain that had to be dealt with before I could pull it out completely. As children and young people without a fully developed frontal lobe, we come to unhealthy conclusions about situations we observe that are simply not true or helpful. It has happened to all of us.

The other thing you must know about the process of pulling weed seeds out of the garden of your mind is that shame will attach itself to you as you finally get to the root of the matter.

> There is no condemnation for those who belong to Christ Jesus because through Christ Jesus the law of the Spirit who gives life has set you free from the law of sin and death. (Romans 8:1–2)

Be authentic with yourself about the lies you believe that are not producing the fruit you want; this is imperative to your breakthrough and learning to walk out your *yes* at varying levels and degrees through life. It is time to start weeding. God has truth and life on the other side of these lies. Take time to quiet your soul in silence and solitude with God. If this is your first time, it might feel awkward, but the Holy Spirit yearns to help you identify these lies that could be keeping you from moving to another place in your relationship with God and in the life that God has marked out for you.

Make It Personal

After you've quieted your mind and heart in solitude, ask God the following question (this is followed by some practice questions to help you discern if you're hearing his voice accurately):

Father, are there any lies that I believe about myself or others that you want to heal?

Listen. What do you hear? Does it line up with God's Word? God's Word is always your litmus test. God is truth, and he cannot contradict his Word.

If you hear a lie, ask Father God if anyone in your life has introduced this lie to you. If someone comes to mind, forgive that person. Say, "Father, I forgive _____ for introducing me to the lie that _____."

_____

_____

_____

_____

Now that you have identified the lie, renounce that lie. For example, "God, forgive me for believing the lie that _____."

Ask God for his truth to replace the thought. "Father, what is the truth?" Rinse and repeat as many times as necessary.

Pace yourself because this is a lifelong process and a tool for the journey. For more resources, check out ConnectUp Ministry.

_____

_____

Do additional lies or thoughts come to mind? Write those down and repeat the steps and questions above.

_____

_____

_____

CHAPTER 10

Through the Valley

The pain of writing this chapter is the very thing that has transformed my life. We may not like to think of Jesus as one who suffered, but he certainly knows our suffering—physically, emotionally, and spiritually. In fact, the Bible tells us there is purpose in our pain if we don't allow it to stop us from moving forward.

> And the God of all grace, who called you to his eternal glory in Christ, after you have suffered a little while, will himself restore you and make you strong, firm and steadfast. (1 Peter 5:10 NIV)

We all try to avoid pain, but pain with a purpose is very powerful. Pain is often the catalyst for long-term change in our lives. Pain that is released to the Father through what Christ did for us on the cross becomes like Lucy's healing ointment in *The Chronicles of Narnia*. A drop of Lucy's healing ointment healed hearts and lives.

I've often seen that the areas that are the most painful in our lives are the areas where God has anointed us to help others with a unique ability to minister to the hearts of others who walk through similar pain. It is only through submitting that pain to Jesus that God turns it into something anointed and supernatural. When we submit our pain, grief, and loss to the Father, he transforms it into a powerful catalyst in our lives. What Jesus did for us on Calvary served as a catalytic converter, of sorts, because his shed blood, through agonizing pain, made a way for us to walk through ours.

His supernatural strength, by way of the Holy Spirit, allows us to grieve and acknowledge the pain with hope and peace. I wish there was another way around the valley of death, but God's Word reminds us that through it is the way we grow, learn, and can be transformed by the renewing of our minds.

The valley of death, or dark night of the soul, comes in different forms for us as believers, based on our unique journeys. For some, it is tragedy, deep loss, or emotional pain from our childhoods that seems to follow us wherever we go, no matter how far we run. The good news is that whoever chooses to lose her life for God's sake will find it.[49]

In extreme cases in some places in the world, some do lose their very lives for the sake of the gospel. These deaths are symbolic of many things, as followers of Christ. We are sure to face certain valleys. *The Pilgrim's Progress* alludes to this in its story of a man who left everything in pursuit of eternity. The first valley of death I remember that shaped my "surrendered yes" to following Christ was when I was around age thirteen. I made the decision to follow Christ with all my heart. I was wrestling with pain in my heart, but as a young teenager, I did not have words for it. I was not mature enough to dig deeper into that pain to understand its root or how to get healed from the inside out. I made a radical commitment to Christ at a tent revival in a country field while sitting on a hay bale. One night at home, I went into my closet to get alone with God and be honest with him—I had taken the minister's instructions to "go into your prayer closet" literally, but I had the first real conversation with God that I can remember clearly.

Although I had no words for the pain I felt in my heart, I gave it to God. I made a promise that I gave to him that night, but later, I ran from it because I didn't fully understand. Nevertheless, God took me up on my promise—"I will follow you through the valley of death." I eventually learned to fear no evil, trusting his rod and his staff to comfort me there, which typically came with some kind of discomfort or form of valley experience. God radically touched my heart and gave me a peace, which I still have no words to describe. I'd always had a tender heart toward God, but I often would project a tough, adventurous, and sometimes rebellious

---

[49] Matthew 10:39.

personality to others. On the inside, though, I was riddled with insecurity, fear, and a desire to please.

When I went to my small country middle school, I had a desire to fit in and be liked. Yet my genuine passion for God and my desire to please him made it hard to do what others wanted me to do, so I decided to stand alone. I found myself at the lunch table of misfits and outcasts and painfully accepted my seat there. My friendship with the girls at that table, however, led them to attend church with me, where they eventually found Jesus for themselves. Somehow, in the valley of death, God makes beautiful things out of hard places. I gave him my yes, and that meant something to me.

Fast-forward through undergraduate college, after which my search for more led me to the Caribbean as a cruise director and to Australia as a wannabe writer. I was certain that I would work in a faith- based nonprofit, sharing and living the gospel internationally, but I ended up obediently going home to my family. My yes to God led me through a personal valley of death with unmet expectations and a rewriting of my version of living my dreams and the paths I imagined taking to get there.

You are familiar with these as well. I went into life with images of jumping from mountaintop to mountaintop with only victory in mind, but those mountaintops are few and far between. There are many more valleys than peaks in life, which allows Christ to transform us along the way. With each valley we walk through, we shed versions of our false selves; eventually, we have to decide to die to the visions of what we had in mind if we truly trust God's lead in our lives. We will enjoy the journey more through the valley of suffering if we accept that it is a part of the process of becoming who Christ has called us to be. He knows the right path for us to take to ultimately become more like him. Every path, which includes a valley of death to something we had in mind, ultimately transforms us if we recognize it and partner with God in the process of surrender. That path is uniquely designed and tailor fitted for each of us! In other cases, God is masterful at making masterpieces of our messes, our poor choices, and our wrong turns. He simply reroutes us.

There is no other way to overcome fear with faith until we walk through the valley of death and choose to fear no evil. This often requires facing off with our greatest fears and doing so with courage.

Courage is not fearlessness; it is faithfulness to keep walking, even when we don't think we can. It is trusting God's hand to lead us, one step at a time.

Now, nineteen years after making an adult decision to allow God to lead me into his vocational call on my life, I am just now starting to see glimpses of what I saw in my heart then. I got here in very different ways than I thought I would, and I thought the route would be filled with less heartache, pain, and disappointment. I also didn't see the fruit of a family of my own, a church family that we would pioneer, or living in the nation's capital in a metro area. I didn't know when God put the beauty and diversity of the nation's culture in my heart that it would lead me here. I had no idea that he would turn my pain into an anointing to help others. I did not know that he would heal my wounds and give me children from my own womb. Frankly, I did not know I could bear such weight and did not know he'd take the strong, tenacious grit I thought was my weakness and use it for good. I didn't know he would take the fear and anxiety and send me into the headwind of the unknown territory, breaking up fallow ground and planting a light!

I am reminded of Jesus's mother, Mary. She was faced with terrifying news and a perceived cultural shadow of death that awaited her after receiving the news that she was pregnant with the Son of God.[50] Cultural shame awaited this thirteen-year-old girl for answering the call of God in her life. She likely feared what her parents, her community, and her fiancé would say about this news, yet she chose to give God her yes. We know that she had a hard time with how, as do many of us when God speaks, but she trusted him with his process. He encouraged her heart by sharing that her cousin Elizabeth also was walking out her yes to God with her pregnancy with John the Baptist. Your yes will cost you your need to be in control of the plan. It will challenge where you put your security. It will scare you to death until you realize that you do not have to fear death. The real death is not walking in the full and abundant life that God had in mind when you were formed in your mother's womb.[51] You are God's Plan A for the world that you are called to reach!

You picked this book up because you are a woman of integrity and

---

[50] Genesis 1:26–38.
[51] Jeremiah 1:5.

fortitude, and you have faced great valleys of death up until now. I believe that God wants you to know that you are not alone. In fact, *many* women have gone before you. You are on the straight and narrow, but the next leg of the journey requires extraordinary courage. You will face some fears you've hoped you would never need to face. This faceoff will usher you into the next season of your life, and it will be nothing like you thought. It will be better because it is beyond the borders of your control or your obsessive need to know the full plan on how to get there. It will challenge what you thought was responsibility as you realize your greatest responsibility is simply to follow the Father's voice and faithfully live out your promise every day. Whether you are writing term papers, studying, changing diapers, or managing your home or a business, you are being refined right where you are. Now that you're aware of it, surrender through the valley of death so you can learn not to fear through it.

I cannot cross this one with you, but I am here to coach you across into the life you desire the most. It is the place where you can swim in the deep ocean of trust that awaits you and see your greatest dreams fulfilled. You might walk into those dreams with more company than you ever imagined as you inspire others to do the same.

Make It Personal

Read aloud Psalm 139:1–6, 13–18 (below). Ask the Father to make this personal to you. Read it slowly and meditate on the places that jump off the page to you. Underline, highlight, and pause if any of these verses speak to you in whatever valley you are facing.

> You have searched me, Lord,
> and you know me.
> You know when I sit and when I rise;
> you perceive my thoughts from afar.
> You discern my going out and my lying down;
> you are familiar with all my ways.
> Before a word is on my tongue
> you, Lord, know it completely.

You hem me in behind and before,
and you lay your hand upon me.
Such knowledge is too wonderful for me,
too lofty for me to attain. ...
For you created my inmost being;
you knit me together in my mother's womb.
I praise you because I am fearfully and wonderfully made;
your works are wonderful, I know that full well.
My frame was not hidden from you
when I was made in the secret place,
when I was woven together in the depths of the earth.
Your eyes saw my unformed body;
all the days ordained for me were written in your book
before one of them came to be.
How precious to me are your thoughts, God!
How vast is the sum of them.
Were I to count them,
they would outnumber the grains of sand—
When I awake, I am still with you.

What verses stood out to you? How is God speaking to you personally through his Word today? Does your heart feel encouraged as you read God's promises toward you?

_____

_____

_____

_____

CHAPTER 11

At the Crossroads

Throughout my experience, I have learned that our Father is a gentleman who will not push his way into our lives. In fact, he will willingly allow us to go around the proverbial mountain as many times as needed until we realize that we must let go of the false selves to step into the truest versions of ourselves. Beneath the surface of our lives are deep, subconscious layers of the false selves we think we need in order to feel successful.[52] The problem is that when those driving forces become the loudest voices in your life, the person you really are is drowned out, and you become less familiar with it. I know this all too well.

On the Enneagram assessment,[53] the classic self-discovery tool, I'm a type three—the Achiever. My drive to achieve has led me on paths that were not my truest self because I was addicted to the achievement fix that comes from accomplishing goals. One gift that God gave me to help temper and train my achiever was marriage and children. It forced me to deal with the deeper root issues and the shadow side of my wiring. Both marriage and children became the catalyst at different levels to help me identify the underlying issues of my life that drove me to achieve affirmation from producing.

Every personality type has its blind spots, but we all have a responsibility to become self-aware enough to manage the tension between our strengths

---

[52] P. Scazzero, "The False Self," Emotionally Healthy Discipleship, June 27, 2013, https://www.emotionallyhealthy.org/the-false-self.
[53] "The Achiever Enneagram Type Three," The Enneagram Institute, January 29, 2023, https://www.enneagraminstitute.com/type-3.

and weaknesses. Many women like me want to do it all in the same season, and while we can do many things, we may not be able to do all of it in every season in the way we plan or desire. For many years, I struggled with my desire to contribute in meaningful ways, make a living to provide for myself, and be a well-balanced, spiritually contemplative spiritual leader while raising a young family. You can see my personality at play that would lead to the belief that I can do all of that at 100 percent.

During a particularly full season, however, I felt the tension growing in my soul's ability to keep up with it all. At some point, we cannot continue to ignore the deep inner voice that will require us to let go of some of the responsibilities that were definitely agreements in one season to create margin for the next. It is in letting go that we give our souls margin to be heard. Even those who thrive on spinning multiple plates, as I do, must yield to God's leading in the crossroads of life, where it is time to take the exit ramp on roads that were once right but can no longer be traveled in the same way. I have learned the hard way to listen to my body, soul, and spirit. It is imperative that you get familiar with your dashboard indicators because your soul will tell you when to shift gears. If you choose to ignore any of the soul cries, which living from some of your false selves may tell you, your body eventually will get your attention as a last resort.

We need to follow God's lead at the crossroads and be willing to shed ourselves of the false selves we try to hold onto when God is leading us in a different direction. As a woman who likes a plan, changing directions can feel like a train wreck for me, rather than a simple off-ramp, preparing me for the next on-ramp.

After the birth of each of my children, I was radically shaken, yet a little more like my true self, even if I was not yet comfortable with the role of mother. I found myself holding on to old versions of myself with a death grip because I had worked so hard to achieve them, and it was too hard to let go of what I knew to embrace the new season into which God was calling me. In ten short years of marriage at the time, I had experienced five moves, the birth of three children (through major surgeries each time), multiple job and role changes, and local church leadership transition. I thrived on change, yet as I got older, something was changing within me, although I could not put words to it then. I did not like change as much as I thought I did, and all the constant pivoting wore on my soul without building proper margin to allow my soul to be heard.

By our third child and the birth of a church, neither of which was in my plan but was glorious eustress, a late onset of postpartum depression, mixed with a mini midlife crisis in my mid-thirties, became unwelcome visitors for which I had not planned or prepared. This curveball was my focal point for the next six to nine months as I fought to get back to my normal, fully functioning self by significantly offloading my responsibilities. Through the process, I came to many crossroads when I felt the spirit of God leading me to willingly exit my full-time employment, which I'd fought to hold on to, even though I felt the spirit of God leading me to let go. As I grappled for months in recovery, I made the decision to say yes to God's journey, even though it continued to look like nothing I had expected. I knew he was asking me to trust him yet again with what seemed much riskier this time, with the weight of a family and church.

His ways are not our ways, and I was trying to hold on to an old version of myself when God was pulling me forward into a new season.[54] As a strong-willed woman, regardless of your personality wrapping, this strength can leave you most vulnerable to missing the leading of the Holy Spirit in your life if your heart is not supple. For me, it often hindered the progress God wanted to make in my spiritual journey when I failed to see his hand leading me to another crossroad. I was reminded of standing at the podium in front of my high school graduating class as the valedictorian, "preaching" about the narrow road and that many do not find it, I had no idea of the prophetic nature of that call to action to my class. I charged my senior class to make every effort to find and travel the narrow road, no matter the cost.[55] I was reminded of the crossroads I found myself facing in that particular season and decided to honor my yes to God again and choose the narrow road of followership. I picked up my own cross in that season.

The wider roads were paved with more perceived security. The other roads were more attractive most of the time than the one to which God often led me, yet he called me to an even narrower road that had my unique name on it, and I was terrified. You, too, might be terrified of the

---

[54] Isaiah 55:8–9.
[55] Matthew 7:13.

narrow road toward which God is leading you. Your job is to follow his lead, seek wise counsel, and take a leap of faith in that direction. He will not let you down. You will look back, years from now, on those leaps and be glad you took them.

> "For my thoughts are not your thoughts, neither are your ways my ways," declares the Lord. "As the heavens are higher than the earth, so are my ways higher than your ways and my thoughts than your thoughts." (Isaiah 55:8–9)

I studied organizational leadership in my master's program in my mid-twenties and knew that titles were not always as they appeared. I knew that I wanted to lead in servant leadership, but the dissonance between what I knew and what I desired was still at war within me. God was calling me to a road of obscurity in my late thirties, and that seemed counter to what I should have been doing at that stage of my life. Can you relate? You thought maybe you'd be married by now, have kids, live in a certain home, or have achieved certain professional accolades by certain milestones in your life. I was forced to grapple with the narrower road to which he was calling me and whether I would choose it. That narrow road was not paved and looked more like a faint trail in the forest that would require an ax to pave a way for others to travel it. That road was less structured than I preferred and came with more risks than I was comfortable with at that season of my life. With my *yes* at that particular time, the opportunities before me felt unpolished and came with nothing more than the satisfaction of doing it for the audience of one in a hiking pack with three small children behind my husband, who I was still learning to trust to lead our family and now a church. The same sin that tempted Eve was tempting me—the pride of wondering if God would hold out on me. Eve was tempted by Satan in the garden with the simple lie that maybe God was holding out on her and that she'd better take care of herself.[56] What if God didn't show up? Death by what-ifs is real! Could God really be trusted? What if I made an unwise decision that would cost me and my family greatly?

---

[56] Genesis 3:1–7.

THE MOST IMPORTANT YES

> Now the serpent was more crafty than any of the wild animals the Lord God had made. He said to the woman, "Did God really say, 'You must not eat from any tree in the garden'?" (Genesis 3:1)

In some ways, I continued to wrestle with the decision to honor my promise to follow God's lead, to come alongside my husband with no backup plan for our lives. I was reminded of a woman of the Bible named Hannah who wrestled with trusting God, yet she did. Hannah wanted a child and remained barren.[57] Hannah was born in a time when it was acceptable for a man to have more than one wife. Her rival housewife was Peninnah, who had no problem with having children. Peninnah rubbed it in and purposefully made it more painful for Hannah. Yet Hannah continued on gritting her way to the house of God, petitioning God for what was in her heart by him. Eventually, she did give birth to a son, Samuel. Samuel was known as the greatest prophet in Israel's history and played a significant role in Bible history. It all started with Hannah's yes to follow God through the pain and to trust him with her desires. I am sure Hannah would tell us that it took far longer than she'd hoped for and that she'd rather not have been teased, provoked, or misunderstood by her husband and priest in the process. Nevertheless, she held on to God with all she had and saw the promise fulfilled. May we be the Hannahs of our generation to carry the promises of God to the next generation by living our story with God and honoring our yeses through all the twists and turns.

As I searched my heart and wrestled in private for months, I knew I needed to let go. I had a support team that couldn't make that decision for me, but they spoke truth and encouraged me to take the road less traveled, as they sensed God was working in my life at the time. There is wisdom in a multitude of advisers; then, you'll ultimately have to make the decision to cross over as you hold on to the covenant you made with God to give him your yes again.

I don't know which crossroad you're facing, but I sense there is a narrow road ahead for you. You will need to remember the agreement you made when you committed your heart and life to Christ. Submit your

---

[57] 1 Samuel 1:2–2:1.

plans, and commit to the process of dying to the false selves that you've erected to protect your version of success. I see a picture of you standing at a crossroad, wanting to please God. The wide road is paved with perceived safer options, yet you know the Holy Spirit is leading you into your next adventure. That may be marriage, kids, or a completely different vocational path. It might be a small pivot, or it might feel like a leap across the Grand Canyon. You were never meant to live a life you could manage on your own or that made sense only by your design. You were never meant to live so small that you could control and engineer it all by yourself. The path of unknown adventure awaits you beyond your ability to plan or control it. Make the choice to allow your commitment of yes to lead you where Father God guides you. His road for you is the path to success and to your authentic self, where you will find fulfillment and rest in God. It will be confusing at first because you will have to die to layers of false self before you recognize yourself again. Who will define your path? Are you willing to reintroduce yourself to you again?

Make It Personal

How did God speak to you in this chapter? What came to mind as you read these words? What is your next yes? What practical steps should you take? Put a time stamp on it, and plan to move forward in obedience.

_____

_____

_____

_____

_____

CHAPTER 12

Hope and New Life

As I sat on a hay bale in the middle of the country-field parking lot of a small church, the country preacher gave an altar call, asking if anyone would like to make a decision to follow Jesus. As a thirteen-year-old, I took those words the preacher spoke back to my bedroom, and I climbed into my closet to do business with God for myself. I was raised in church, and the local church was at the epicenter of my upbringing, but this was the first time I made a decision for myself to "pick up my cross" and follow Jesus. Of course, I chose again, ten years later as a young adult, to pick up that cross as I tried to find my own way in the world. I internally wrestled with what I thought I wanted and a desire to make a difference in the world in the way that only I could. I deeply desired to live a life of significance, and I thought—for a long time—that I had to pick up my cross and strive apart from Christ to find that way. I am not entirely sure where this dualistic thinking entered my mind, but the two were very much intertwined.

As an independently raised woman, that toughness served me well, until it did not. Somewhere along the way, I picked up a lie that it was not OK to depend on anyone to lead me. Rather, I behaved as if God was more like an accessory of faith instead of the primary driver of my life, which would lead me to places I would rather not go. In fact, picking up my cross would require death to the things and timing I had in mind, which I had to surrender if I wanted to truly live my best life.[58] It would require dying

---

[58] J. Osteen, *My Best Life* (Stratford, VA: Faith Works Publishing, 2004).

to the images I'd erected of what I deemed successful and would require a stripping and surrendering of my hard-charging adventurous spirit to the potter's wheel of God's art room again.

Have you ever used a tool or utensil for a purpose for which it was not intended? It will work, but it looks funny because it was not designed to do that particular task. You may not get the intended results, and it is simply harder than it should be. That is a lot like our lives. We can make anything work—relationships, jobs, or even the pants that don't really fit right! There is no discomfort like wearing pants all day that are just too tight; it will make you grumpy after a while. We have a lot of grumpy people going through the motions of what they think is success, but they have not consulted their custom designer for what he had in mind. He has a tailormade life designed for you, if you are courageous enough to depart from the well traveled path with clear signage and paved roads. It will not look like others because it is specifically designed for you, and you are a designer's original. When you look at your life that way, it seems silly to compare your journey to others' journeys.

You are probably familiar with Noble Prize winner Mother Teresa. To many, her path of success looked like the way down. She spent her life serving the poor in the streets of Calcutta, India. Her surrender to God's path of success looked very different than what many of us may dream of as a successful life, yet she set a new bar for what living a meaningful life looks like. Mother Teresa left teaching high school girls in the convent to go to the streets outside those windows. Some wondered why she would leave the comfort of her convent to live among the people, yet her *yes* to the calling of God meant more to her than the well-laid plans for a successful path in life. She pioneered her own path and made history. She started open-air schools for the overlooked and forgotten. She started the Missionaries of Charity to fund the work of caring for the vulnerable and forgotten in the slums of Calcutta. I would say that her yes cost her much more than she thought it would, but it was more fulfilling and successful than she imagined it would be when she decided to follow God's leading.[59]

The only way to find the true life God has called you to live or to pioneer is with a proverbial death of some sort to what you had in mind. It requires you to die to some of the images of success you've erected in

---

[59] M. T. Bojaxhiu, *No Greater Love* (Novato, CA: The New World Library, 2002).

your life and to follow the narrow road that God has marked out for you. Then, when the enemy tries to resurrect those old versions of your false self, you must carry a nail and hammer in your pocket. The closer you get to your true self, the more fear you will face because the enemy comes to steal, kill, and destroy. He is the father of lies wrapped in fear because he fears nothing more than your realizing who you really are—a daughter of the King of kings![60] You will realize that nothing is impossible for you as you partner with the voice of God in your life.

The devil will resist you at every turn because the scariest thing to him is the havoc of which a Holy Spirit–filled woman of God is capable when she dies to what she had in mind and embraces her cross—the cross God called her to bear—with willingness, surrender, and meekness. She is powerful in God. That is you, my dear sister. I hope, as you read these words, that the love of God embraces you like a warm hug as you muster the courage to follow where he leads you. Abraham laid Isaac, his dream, on the altar and trusted God to provide.[61] This is a necessary passageway to life in the kingdom of God. He knows what you need. He knows the desires of your heart. He knows what you have sacrificed to follow him, and you will not be ashamed of following his lead.[62]

"No one who hopes in you will ever be put to shame."

There is a real temptation that I call a religious spirit that lurks in everyone's life. Somehow, when we give God our yes and enter a faith relationship with Him, we start trying to climb the ladder of earning His approval. The longer we walk with God, the more grace-filled we should become, as we will realize that we receive the gift of God through grace by faith. This means we can't earn more of his love, acceptance, or approval. We were already signed, sealed, and delivered in his image, as approved by him. When we say yes to God, we accept that truth, and we live from it, not for it! In this revelation, we should become painfully aware of our need for God and the enemy's tactics to tempt us in the same areas of weakness,

---

[60] John 8:44.
[61] Genesis 22:1–19.
[62] [62] Psalm 25:3a.

over and over again. We should grow more aware and confident that we can do nothing without God, but with him, anything is possible.

I never would have imagined that I would have a family of five and a dog in the nation's capital or that I'd be coleading a church with my husband. That was not on my radar, yet here I am. In some ways, the death in comparison and to the images I thought were true for my life had to be deconstructed before I could embrace the true purpose and calling that God placed on my life. I would pray as a young teenager that I would walk in the original purpose and plan God had for my life. I had no idea what I was praying for, and I certainly did not think it would take forty plus years of continual sculpting to get me to a place where I was ready to lead from my authentic self.

A couple years into marriage, after the birth of our first child, I had a dream that awoke me to the real struggle going on in my heart at that time. As a strong, interdependent woman now, I can share this dream with much confidence that it was God instructing me in the night, even when I did not realize it. I had a dream that my husband was in the driver's seat of our car, and I was in the passenger seat, with our oldest (then the only child) in her infant car seat in the back. We appeared to be in the Shenandoah Mountains on a winding road, and we were fighting—I wanted to drive, and I kept trying to take the wheel from him. Eventually, I caused us to drive off a cliff. The car went off the road and over the edge. Jesus came into the car and told me to politely let go of the wheel and get in the back with my daughter, for our safety. I was not only terrified but mortified that I caused the accident. He told me he would sit in the driver's seat and help Jeremy steer this family in this next season.

I knew that God needed me to relinquish control of some specific areas at the time and tend to my daughter, following Jeremy's lead. I did not like it, but Jesus's kindness led me to repentance.[63] I woke up from the dream and thought that I needed to change. I needed to deal with the deep-seated mistrust I had with God and my husband. The deeper issue was a struggle over control and authority. I was afraid to submit my life to someone else and allow my husband to lead me. It was hard enough to allow God to lead me, much less another person.

That dream changed my life and sent me on a journey of picking up

---

[63] Romans 2:4.

my cross in this area of leadership and trust. Picking up our cross is not a one-time decision; it is a lifelong journey of many decisions to surrender, until we see Jesus face to face. We can do it our way, but it likely will leave us hanging over a cliff in a mess! I often wonder why God made me so strong willed, but then I realize that the same strong will has helped me to make hard decisions in life to keep following Jesus. The same is true for you. God has given you an inner strength to do the hard things and follow where he leads you. Your path is different from mine, but the principle remains the same. Will you trust him to lead you through the crossroads, to pick up your cross and follow? Why has God given you the strength, the grit, and the fortitude that he has? Is it for your glory or his? We are the daughters of Sarah, the great matriarch of our faith, who was called to step out into the land that God would show them. That took strength and fortitude; it took grit. And we are her daughters. That same grit that Sarah had from the Lord lives in you! The power of the Holy Spirit empowers you to do the hard things. We have her story to guide us and gain wisdom from her mistakes of rebellion and mistrust and her lack of submission to God's plan. If Sarah was here, I believe she'd want us to learn through her story so we might trust God with quick obedience and follow him where he leads without a fight.[64]

Make It Personal

Take a moment to talk to God before moving forward. Ask him if there are any areas of rebellion or mistrust in your life that he wants to reveal. Practice listening prayer by quieting yourself and waiting quietly in his presence to speak to your spirit. Ask him if there is a specific lie that you believe that has led you to rebel or mistrust his leadership.[65]

---

[64] Genesis 1–11.
[65] L. Payne, *Listening Prayer* (Ada, MI: The Baker Publishing Group, 1999).

Write down that lie so you can see it. Ask God if anyone introduced you to this lie. If someone comes to mind, simply forgive that person or persons from your heart.[66]

___

Break agreement with the lie you've identified out loud. There is something powerful about hearing yourself acknowledge and break agreement with the lie that has been holding you captive to sinful thinking, holding you back from experiencing true freedom!

Ask the Father what the truth is or what he wants to give you in exchange. Thank him for it.

___

[66] K. & M. Luse, *Connect Up Training Manual* (Harrisburg, PA: Connect Up Ministries, 2018).

CHAPTER 13

Hindrances, Lies, and Transformation

To put it bluntly, you have an enemy, as has every other woman who has gone before you. The enemy wants nothing more than to sell you lies that keep you from experiencing the freedom that Christ died to give you. The Bible is very clear about his intentions. Through Jesus, we are able to live an abundant life of inner freedom and become everything God had in mind on this side of heaven. Change-management theory suggests that change happens at the individual level first. In fact, if we are going to change anything with the Holy Spirit's help, it will require our awareness and desire first. I want to remind you that you have an enemy of your soul. The enemy prowls around like a lion, seeking whoever he may devour.[67] His mission is to mar the image of God that you reflect on the earth. You reflect your Creator, whom he loathes. We also have the ability to give life to other human beings who reflect God's image. Christ defeated the enemy once and for all, but the real battle is with whose image we will reflect in the earth through the influence God has given us as women. The most important work we can do is to actively remove the hindrances that keep us from putting on the mind of Christ and thinking like our Father. Lies are the hindrances we pick up along life's journey of disappointments, fears, and wounds, which happen as a result of being human. Christ died to give us a choice on whose report

---
[67] 1 Peter 5:8.

we will believe about those things. We face off with what author Mark Batterson called the three-headed dragon of shame, fear, and control that are entangled with lies. All of these become hindrances to living the abundant life Christ has in mind for all of us.

I wish I could tell you that once you commit your life to Jesus with your wholehearted *yes*, life will somehow get easier, but that is not the case. You simply become a greater threat to the kingdom of darkness. Sometimes, I think the temptations become all the more targeted. The enemy of your soul, the devil, is masterful at tailormade battles that are aimed at stealing your breath. Some of life's challenges are meant to discourage you and tempt you to question if God is really good. They may cause you to hide in shame, act in fear, and even idolize and act for perceived control. The temptations come from the same lie that Eve believed when she was tempted in the garden of Eden. Is God really good, or is he holding out on me? Can I trust him and his ways? The enemy tricked Eve into believing that God was holding out on her and that going her own way was a better route. Anyone who has forced her own way often will tell of the pain and suffering that eventually came as a result of pressing for her own way. I want to unveil a couple of tactics that your enemy, Satan, will use to steal, kill, and destroy your ability to abide in God's perfect will for your life, which is staying close to his heart.

As a former high school basketball player, I am going to call the enemy's tactic to steal, kill, and destroy you his *triple threat* or the three-headed dragon you must slay to live victoriously in Christ. It is a customized thorn to your flesh that brings discouragement, doubt, and fear into your heart at all the vulnerable places of your life. The enemy of your soul will exploit past hurts and wounds in your life without mercy. He is masterful at hitting us in our blind spots and whispering lies in the place of discouragement. When I'm aware of the schemes of the enemy, I am better positioned to go on the offense so I can thwart his plan against me and my family. The Bible doesn't call him a father of lies without reason. He is the chief marketer of sin (no offense to those in the marketing field). As an undergraduate marketing major, I learned there is a tailored plan that is targeted at selling you anything and everything, whether you need it or not, based on your subjective likes and dislikes. The enemy is the same way.

It may be that your need for people-pleasing approval and acceptance will cause you to compromise your character and deepest convictions. It may be the deep-seated desires of your heart, out of God's timing, that the enemy will tempt you to sell short of God's best for your life, such as marrying the wrong person or taking a job that doesn't bring you peace, even with a great salary and benefits. He will always prey on your weaknesses to expose your vulnerability. It is maddening to realize how low he will go to divinely set you up to fail and fall into an entanglement of sin, as he sells it as culturally acceptable. There are practical things you can do to be on guard against the enemy's schemes as he prowls around like a lion, seeking someone to devour (1 Peter 5:8). Author C. S. Lewis brilliantly depicts the spiritual warfare that happens around us in his masterpiece *The Screwtape Letters*. If we are to overcome the enemy's vicious attacks in our lives, with his ultimate goal of marring our perception and relationship with God, we must know a few truths so we can fight for the victory that God says is already ours as his daughters.

First, know who God really is. You learn who God is by reading his Word and learning about his character. It is imperative that you can discern who God *is* and *is not* so you can distinguish to whose voice you are listening.

Second, know yourself, your temptations, and the personal blind spots of your nonstrengths so that you do not unintentionally fall into sinful patterns that the enemy will use to trap you. For example, my sincere love for people and the strength of always hoping and seeing the best in people can be naive and people-pleasing, which can cause me a lot of heartache and unnecessary anxiety. Are you looking to please and follow God or to seek the approval of others?

Third, look for the open doors where you might have bought some lies about who you think you are or what you think you must do for God's approval versus what God requires of you. The only thing he has required of you without pressure is to do justly, love mercy, and walk humbly with your God.[68] What additional bricks have you loaded into your backpack, and what is the fruit of all the weight you have been carrying? Has it led to more joy or peace?

---

[68] Micah 6:8.

Fourth, once you've identified those lies as the enemy's lies, renounce or break agreement with those lies immediately. Ask for forgiveness and repent. Forgive anyone along the way who might have introduced those lies, and seek the truth. Turn the other way, and ask God what the truth is. Begin to live and make decisions from that newly established truth. For example, a common lie women believe is that we are not good enough or that whatever we do is not good enough. It seems innocent enough, but this is incredibly destructive and will bear fruit like striving, overperformance, approval-seeking that leads to integrity-value compromise, and an inability to rest in the love of God, which leads to exhaustion and poor decisions. It seems so innocent, but one simple lie wedged in our heart can give birth to a host of bad fruit in our mind. Break agreement with the lie, and ask God what the truth is instead. Test that truth with the Word of God, and ensure that it aligns with his character and his Word. Rinse and repeat one thousand-plus times for the rest of your life.

Slowly, we are transforming into image bearers of our Father. As we get the hang of it, we will take some sisters along with us on this journey toward freedom and fulfillment! We will use our influence to help other women get free too and become all that God had in mind for them as well. Our mandate, as God's daughters, is to be confident and secure in our Father's love and so that we can bear his image on the earth in the many ways we do that, day to day.

Another hindrance that needs to be removed and remodeled is the temptation to compare. We naturally compare and compete, but this is not God's best for us. The sooner we accept that God has a unique plan for each of us, the closer we will be to finding true contentment and joy in our own personal journeys with him. We rob ourselves of the joy and fulfillment that comes from being our authentic selves.

If you value success and are wired for action with some drive in your personality, this will be vitally important for you. You will need to make the decision to stop comparing and benchmarking your journey against others. Make the decision to celebrate others instead, and choose to propel others forward, as you are able. You don't need to compare yourself to anyone else! God has a unique path for you if you will say yes to the adventure with him. I often tell my children to take a long, hard look at their fingerprints. No one else in the world has their unique fingerprint, even if it looks similar to others.[69] My dad taught me that. A transformative process begins to happen within us when we choose to purposefully celebrate others. We pave new neurological pathways for a new way of thinking and living by God's design for us. For example, when your "sister friend" gets into that doctorate program, marries her soul mate, has a baby, or finally lands her dream job, you purposefully decide to go out of your way to celebrate her and suffocate any comparison and jealousy you may feel.

What you feed grows, and what you starve dies. Don't feed the flesh of comparison that causes you to undermine appreciation for your own uniqueness. Comparison and jealousy are not who you really are! It is the fruit of your flesh, which comes with being fully human. God has a unique journey for you, and it will look nothing like your sister friend's journey. It will be unique to you, with God's timeline for your life and his divine purpose for you! You will only answer to him and be accountable for *your* yes, not your neighbor's yes.

My parents owned horses in my childhood, and sometimes, it was necessary to put blinders on the horses to keep them focused on the step in front of them without being distracted. There are seasons when you may need to put on your own blinders to stay focused on the lane of life that God has called you to live for the audience of one. He wants you to get your eyes off the super homeschool mom across the street, the CEO executive around the corner and her world travels, or the friend who seems to have it all. It is so easy to get distracted by someone else's call, when the only thing God has asked you to do is to follow his lead and trust him with your own journey. Now that you are aware of the hindrances in becoming the truest version of yourself, you must decide to do the hard work of renewing your mind daily with every opportunity and with intentionality. It will take courage to do the inner work necessary to really honor your yes to Jesus.

I implore you to do some introspection with God and take inventory of which areas you may be prone to compare. If you have a biblically centered spiritual director, counselor, pastor, or sister to invite along on your journey to share your experiences, invite them to play a role in this next season for support and encouragement. We all need accountability and someone to process with us as we commit to this transformational way of life in Christ.

---

[69] R. Foster, *Celebration of Discipline: The Path for Spiritual Growth* (New York, NY: Harper Collins, 2009).

A couple of years ago, God gave me an invitation during a time that felt dark and scary to me. Some may even define it as a dark-night-of-the-soul type of experience. I had been running hard professionally during a decade full of change and transformation for our family. I was coming out of the postpartum period with our third child, and I was exhausted—mentally, physically, and psychologically. I was thirty-seven when I hit a brick wall that no amount of prayer, reading, silence, or coaching could get me over or through. My life came to a halt.

One morning, I woke up and, for the first time in my life, I had no motivation to continue. I felt numb inside, and my body began to detox from the adrenaline and stress I had carried all my life, leaving me restless at night and shaking in my bed, with racing thoughts that felt like a train coming full speed ahead. My husband and I decided to launch a church after a decade of running hard in the marketplace, serving in our local church, having children, and making a lot of life adjustments. After the birth of our third child, with two toddlers at home, and working full time outside the home, in addition to the new church venture, I had found my limits. I sat on the floor, nursing my child, while working on the backend of the church through my maternity leave. I ignored all the dashboard indicators that were blinking for my attention physically, emotionally and spiritually. I didn't rest well during my short leave; I was riddled with anxiety about the preparations that had to be made and expanded so I could come back, full steam ahead, with my employer, as well as devote full weekends to the church. I had left no margin for myself in the equation. I began to hear the voice of God lovingly prepare me for a transition with my employer, but I was not ready to let go. I was not willing to let go of anything because I found security in my over-functioning. Why couldn't I continue to do everything I was doing at the same intensity that I'd done it before? Wasn't everything possible with God? My body, mind, and soul began to cry out louder and louder until it got my attention physically and emotionally. My physical body was the part of me that decided to stop functioning properly, which indicated the type of internal stress I was carrying. Although I didn't realize it, the weight had shifted in my life. The circumstances had changed significantly, and I had not changed with them. I needed to adjust the weight for a season to regain my balance, but I refused.

A group fitness coach told me I needed to downshift the weight in a new exercise that required me to use underdeveloped muscles, and I did not want to. Sometimes, the coach needs us to adjust our weight in certain seasons until we develop different muscles to carry the weight.

I held on a little longer, and for three more months, I wrestled deeply inside. Every day felt as if I was recovering again from major surgery, but this time, it was holistic. God was putting his finger on something much deeper than a cesarean scar. God began to speak to me about the inner work he wanted to do and that it was time for a change. I had to deal with some lies that resurfaced about the false responsibility I had carried to this point in chronic overworking, overstretching, and the lack of margin for true stillness inside. My soul longed for true solitude that would heal my broken body, soul, and spirit fully, after such a hard decade of running. It was as if I acknowledged the limitations of this human shell, which I internally despised. After six months of counseling, writing, journaling, and detoxing from chronic stress and adrenal fatigue, I acknowledged the root of over-functioning and overproducing. It manifested itself in overworking, overthinking, overplanning, and lack of rest. The good news is that when I finally decided to stop resisting the holistic healing process with humility, I acknowledged that I had pushed myself too hard for too long, and it was time to yield. It was time to learn a different way of living and leading at a new level of weight in life. It was time to understand what Jesus said when he told us that his yoke is easy and his burden is light.[70] He was asking me to cast my cares upon him, for he cared for me. The truth is that I believed I was the source of my strength until I couldn't be anymore. With the support of spiritual accountability, a counselor, doctor, friends, and my family, I was able to heal and change for the better. I finally slowed down inside, and that began my healing process.

Author and pastor John Mark Comer writes:

> To restate: love, joy, and peace are at the heart of all Jesus is trying to grow in the soil of your life. And all three are incompatible with hurry. The solution to an over-busy life

---

[70] Matthew 11:28–30.

is not more time. It's to slow down and simplify our lives around what really matters.[71]

I had to slow down to locate where I was and to get my body, soul, and spirit back into alignment and to adjust to the weight that God was calling me to in that season of my life.

Sarah, Abraham's wife, was finally confronted with her lack of trust in God after a long journey of disappointment, pain, and wounds, having followed Abraham into the desert as a barren woman. Three men, believed to be angels, visited Abraham and prophesied the promised child Isaac after twenty five years of disappointment. Sarah was in the tent and overheard the conversation. She laughed in disbelief that God would now honor her after she was worn out, old, and tired of doing everything on her own to make it happen. Sarah lied to cover the shame she felt when she was confronted; hence, we see an invitation for Sarah to look within at this moment.[72] Could it be that she prolonged the entire journey by her inability to trust and her taking things into her own hands to make it happen? Was the real issue that she simply did not trust God's ways or his timing? We all have moments, just as the matriarch of our faith did, when we become aware that we need to change. We desire true transformation as we learn to trust God's ways and resist the urge to take matters into our own hands. This is an invitation to slow down and take an internal look at what is going on under the surface of your life. Daughter, God is calling you to a much deeper and meaningful life with him. His yes will lead you to grapple with all the stuff you have kept deep within the recesses of your heart. This is an invitation to slow down and to unpack what is going on under the surface of your life so you can continue to honor your first yes—to keep following God where he leads you in the chapters ahead. Take time to identify the hindrances that may be preventing you from moving forward. Which lies hold those hindrances in place? Decide today to take inventory before you hit the wall, as I did; save yourself some pain. Make a goal to do thirty, sixty, ninety day detox of your thought life. Evaluate the deep seeded beliefs in your heart that may be driving your

---

[71] J. M. Comer, *The Ruthless Elimination of Hurry* (New York City, NY: The Crown Publishing Group, 2019).
[72] Genesis 17–18.

daily decisions. Submit those to God in prayer and repent for the works of the flesh that are not his best. Recommit your yes to him with a freshness to do the work that he wants to do in you. Take a moment to make this actionable before you read on.

Make It Personal

Find a quiet place to have some time alone with God. Get something to write on in addition to your book, in preparation for hearing from Him. He longs to speak to you right where you are! That might be your bedroom closet, bathroom floor, or a porch. Those have been my go-to alone spots in my home for many years now, with small children, but you might have a quiet apartment to yourself. Whatever your circumstances, remove all excuses and prioritize it. Clear your calendar in half-hour increments at first. Sitting in stillness takes practice. Your Father longs for you to make the space to be present with him and do a deep work in your heart.

What lies have you believed about God or yourself? Write those down here. You will need to rinse and repeat this daily over time, as you learn a new way of thinking and living the authentic life that God is calling you to live as God's daughter.

For each lie you discover, take a moment to repent, and ask Father God to tell you the truth. By way of Jesus, you have complete access to approach his throne with confidence.[73] He's been waiting on you for a long time.

_____

_____

_____

_____

---

[73] Hebrews 4:16.

In which areas of your life do you constantly compare?

Write those down, and then purposefully give each one to God, and be silent. Ask God what he might have for you, instead of that which you are comparing. Pay attention to the small, still whisper in your heart or even a picture you might see. Be sure to write that down to remind yourself when that area of comparison and jealousy rears its ugly head.

_____

_____

_____

_____

CHAPTER 14

Fear Is a Liar

If you have not experienced it already, your walk with Jesus will require you to face off with the giant of fear. In fact, God's Word refers to us as Sarah's daughters, the matriarch of our faith. She had to face off with the fear of never bearing her own son and leaving the safety and security of what she knew at the ripe age of seventy-five years old. God called them at the age that many deem as a time to be retired into the greatest adventure of their lifetime.

If we unpacked the lives of the women of the Bible, we would see some sort of faceoff with fear in order for them to follow the path and plans God had for their lives. Behind your deepest fears are puzzles, pieces of destiny that you must discover with the help of the Holy Spirit. My yes to God would lead me to many places of surrender. Quite possibly the biggest fear was marriage, family, and motherhood. *Sheer terror* describes the fear that gripped my heart in this area. I feared many things about marriage and motherhood. I attended a prayer ministry session at my local church, where I received a prophetic picture of my future that included my children. I had to wrestle with God because I had allowed fear to disqualify me and had settled for what I pictured for myself. The path on which God was calling me required more domestication and laying down of my life than I ever imagined, yet God has worked through it all, forming me more and more into his image, which is the goal for all of us.

The struggle to surrender my body, soul, and mind to this process of family, to include pregnancy and becoming a mother, was an internal battle. On the other side of surrender, God formed something in me that reflected much more of the Father than if I had stopped giving him my yes at the door of the greatest fear. Every woman wonders if she is enough to be a mother or if she has what it takes to die daily to self and serve those in her house without end. My flesh was holding on to fear as the excuse for following God where he was calling me. The beautiful thing about facing off with the giants of fear is that you realize the indescribable and intangible beauty of trusting God through the wall of fear and into a field of inner freedom.

God wants us to live a life of freedom, and it only exists beyond the facade of the false selves we erect at places of pain in our lives, which once protected us and served a function. The problem becomes the lies that get fortified in our minds and hearts that keep those walls up well beyond the purpose we intended. It is the courage to go beyond the great barriers of fear, where fear is turned into faith, that the real adventure begins. Father God invites us all into a great adventure, but it will most definitely require our faith.

It was with my firstborn daughter, Hanna, that God gave me true inner freedom from some of the lies and fears that had kept me living smaller than he'd called me to live and that caused me to disqualify myself from motherhood. The first time I held my daughter in my arms, after facing off with the fear of a C-section, I realized the pain was worth it. She was the catalyst in my life to do the deep digging on issues of identity about being a Christian woman. As I held my daughter, I realized I did not want her to ever question her identity or to see limits because of her gender but rather to embrace her design to display an aspect of God that only she could! I wanted her to know that God chose her and formed her in my womb just the way she is, and he loves everything about her, even her rough edges. I wanted her to know she had a place in the house of God with whatever gifts God placed in her. I did not want her to ever be disqualified, because she was a woman, from anything that was in her heart from God. I did not want her to have to learn how to "code" in the world to appear a strong leader in various crowds, just to fit in. I wanted her to know it was OK to be an adventurer with great talents and skills to make the world better but also to see the value in having a family of her own without the pressure to choose between the two.

Somehow, I'd picked up on some cultural lies that my gifts had a certain box and place, as a Christian woman. I thought I had to go outside of my faith to be appreciated for the gifts and talents that God gave me. I thought I had to prove myself. I thought I had to work ten times harder than a man, just to get a seat at the table, and to strip myself of all emotion. I thought I was weak if I decided to marry. I thought I could not fulfill the calling of God in my life as well as have kids, as if they were two opposing things when they are both very godly and holy desires! All of these lies had built a fortress of fear that I had to face if I was going to live the full adventure to which God was calling me.

I credit my husband, Jeremy, for seeing the call of motherhood and leading me into the calling of family. That very fear that held me back was a sure sign that the enemy hoped I'd never realize how powerful my yes would be if I turned that fear into faith. As I allowed God to do the deep work beneath the surface of my life, I saw my three children as fiery arrows in my quiver who will wreak havoc on the enemy.

> Like arrows in the hand of a warrior, So are the children
> of one's youth. (Psalm 127:4)

God turned my mourning into dancing and my fear into faith for the impossible. I am a living testament to what God can do, if you'll trust him to lead you where you may be too fearful to go in your flesh. Be led by your spirit, and trust me when I tell you that you will not be disappointed. He knows you better than you know yourself! He is aware of the deepest desires of your heart that you don't even know.

> No one who hopes in the Lord will ever be put to shame.
> (Psalm 25:3)

Make It Personal

What is one of the biggest fears that you are facing off with, even as you read this? Just taking a step to identify it and write it down will disempower the enemy's grip! That is the very area in which God wants to give you freedom. If there are any areas of fear you want to heal, ask Father God.

You may be taken back to a memory. Ask Jesus where he was and what he wants you to give him in that picture. Often, myriad negative thoughts and emotions may flood your body. Your body does keep score and tells you a story, if you are willing to listen.

A picture or word may come to your mind immediately. Explore that with God by asking, "Is there a lie that I believe about you, myself, or a particular event that happened in my life?" Break agreement with that lie, and ask God for the truth.

_____

_____

_____

Take a moment to pray the following with all of your heart:

> Father, I repent for allowing the spirit of fear in this particular area to "eat my lunch." I break agreement with the lie that _____. I ask you to fill my heart with faith in this area, and let me in on the plans you have for me.
>
> Come in faith, expectant, because God longs to commune and talk with us.

What do you hear? What do you see? Write it down, and ponder it in your heart, as Mary did You will need it for the adventure that awaits you from here.

_____

_____

_____

CHAPTER 15

Tackling Shame Head-On

For the longest time, I did not realize that my desire to succeed and appear successful was tied to my design as an achiever who desired to please people. While those traits can be good at times, they also could become the roadblock that could keep me from being my authentic self. As a young college graduate, I was borderline obsessed with finding my way and succeeding, as if it was a ladder of steps. After graduation and many doors closed to opportunities and entry-level jobs, I realized this was not the route I wanted to take. I questioned religion and was on a mission to discover my purpose.

I boarded a plane after receiving an offer to be an activities mate. I later found out the job was that of a full-blown cruise director, including managing everything to do with people's experience aboard this tall ship, part of a family-owned small fleet of tall ships based out of Miami that sailed the Caribbean. Every day was full of multiple jobs, in which I thrived as a young, ambitious, energetic young woman. After completing a one-year contract and with relative success and exhaustion, I was offered a job in Sydney, Australia, in events, with the promise to be mentored in the area of writing. Without doing proper research, I boarded the plane to Australia with confidence that I would probably never return home.

I was determined to succeed and was sure this opportunity could lead me there. Maybe I would even marry a handsome Aussie adventurer. It did not take long to realize that I did not want to write about the topics in this Australian magazine; I found it to be in conflict with my deepest values. I wrestled with God as I realized that I'd never consulted him on taking this adventure. I tried to numb the ache inside and fit in with my colleagues, but I just did not fit in. As a twenty-two-year-old woman, I put so much pressure on myself to have a plan and succeed at achieving my life purpose and career path that it sent me to my knees. I knew I couldn't stay but was unwilling to admit it yet.

I happened to arrive when the team was getting ready to go on a vision retreat to Bali. My boss asked me to use my cruise director skills to organize some team-building fun, and that is what I did. I arranged biking tours in the countryside of Bali, surf lessons, massages on the beach, and exercise classes. While it was fun, I felt an emptiness inside as I sought to do something more meaningful. I wanted to write about things that mattered. The dissonance grew in my heart over a compromise of my internal values. The conviction of the Holy Spirit grew also, as I continued to fit in, and it finally came to a head. I was sitting on the Indian Ocean under a cabana, with my journal and Bible in hand, when I clearly discerned the voice of God calling me home. I walked into town to the internet cafe and wrote home to my parents. I was humiliated. I vowed that I would not come back until I had found what I was looking for.

Little did I know that the journey was not yet over. Interestingly, I told God that if I was to go home, I needed confirmation. I was specific about the sign I needed, telling God that my boss would have to give me permission to go home. I was invited to a private lunch with my boss, which for other employees was a professional-development coaching session; for me, it was the clarity I needed to go home.

Before I said anything to my boss, she said, "Kristina, you're really good at what you do, but I don't know that you fit in here. You're welcome to stay, but I sense you have a greater purpose and something more meaningful to do with your life. You are free to go when your temporary work visa is up. I will pay you for the work you've done if you choose to leave."

My jaw dropped, and I knew I had heard from God; he was directing my path. I called my father for advice on how to finish my month in Australia, and he encouraged me to explore. I had no idea that the next two weeks of exploration would mark my life forever! I felt lost, and none of the opportunities I chased seemed to be good fits for me. I decided to attend a young-adult church service in Australia one night. As I walked in, I felt like I had come home. Before the altar call was given, I found myself weeping at the front on my knees. The pastor began to describe a young woman who sounded a lot like me, and I couldn't help but think maybe God was speaking through this man to my heart. Someone laid hands on my head as I wept at the altar; I felt ashamed and marked by a failure to launch or find my way in the world. The pastor spoke words of life over me, and I hung on every word he said. I'd been voted most likely to succeed in high school and felt I could not live up to the title. In fact, I'd felt quite the opposite since graduating college.

That night, I was filled with a fresh anointing of the Holy Spirit, and the presence of God made my body tremble as I wept for hours after the service. I returned to my hotel room that evening, still weeping, and crawled into the bathtub. I felt so alone and too far from my family to call them. The shower water washed over me for what seemed like hours as I felt the tangible presence of God, almost a hand resting on my back. I felt the weight of my sin being washed away, and I became a different person. I stood up, touched by the consuming fire of God, with a transformed desire to seek God for the purposes and plans he had. I relinquished the control of doing it on my own.

The next day, I left my hotel room for a week-and-a-half journey, bringing a backpack, a change of clothes, and my Walkman CD player. I camped in outdoor hostels in the Daintree Rainforest in Cairns, Australia, alone with God and nature. In the middle of May, I eventually found myself on the last leg of my backpacking journey. I was on Fitzroy Island, sitting on the white sand, watching sharks and jellyfish frolic together, when I had a conversation with God that changed the trajectory of my life. I pulled out a sisterhood CD that I'd picked up, on which the speaker asks the question: "Who are you?" I broke down crying because I couldn't answer that question. I then discovered the voice of God, as I heard, *"You are a daughter of the most-high God, and I am well pleased with you."*

My identity was settled, and I made a vow to the Lord that day that I would spend the rest of my days discovering what that meant and following wherever he would lead. I gave him my yes again. Although I had tried to do things on my own, God never left me alone. He never meant for me to figure that out alone or to do it apart from him. That day, I knew that the only way I would find the true purpose of my life was to keep giving

God my yes and to follow him where he led. The comfort, presence, peace, and protection I felt that day was where I wanted to live. I did not want anything else. The weight of shame washed off me as I chose to be authentic with God about my feelings of inadequacy, failure, disappointment, and regret. I took him up on the great exchange I knew was possible and gave him permission to start the reforming process that the guy on the ship in Grenada prophesied—he had told me that God, as the potter, wanted to reform the vessel he had made me to be so I could fulfill the purposes he intended for my life.

And that is where I got on the potter's wheel and gave God permission to restore me to his original purpose and design. It also was there that the work began, and I was awakened to the fact that the enemy wants to steal, kill, and destroy purpose, while Jesus came to establish his purposes in us. I learned that I had to face off with the spirit of shame, fear, and control when it reared its ugly head. This three-headed monster was out to confuse and destroy me, and I had to go on the offense. You are not exempt from this battle either. You, too, reflect your Father's image, and therefore, you become a target for the lies and deception that lead you to settling for a life that is less than what God intended.

As I stepped off the plane in my hometown, I sensed and felt the shame of failure. I chose to embrace the opposite spirit to combat the shame I felt. I chose the way of humility and submission to the Father's ways, and I returned to my literal father's house as a twenty-three-year-old single woman. My parents rolled out the red carpet for me with a freshly remodeled room. I spent the next several months praying, studying, and seeking direction until some God doors opened at a Christian college; I was to do exactly what I did *not* enjoy—business administrative clerical work behind a desk under fluorescent lights. Those were the same sales-and-marketing fluorescent lights that had been in an office I'd run from after graduating college. This time, however, I had a purpose for sitting under them.

Although my flesh was opposed to the idea, as I compared it to the desk and the views I'd had eighteen months earlier of Sydney and the Caribbean Sea, I remembered my commitment to follow God where he led. I had many conversations with God at that desk, and he taught me many things. I earned another bachelor's degree, this one in applied theology, while I was there and learned a lot about myself and the gifts God had given me. This continued the reshaping and restoration process as I submitted myself to the potter's wheel, which was my life. As I made copies of student papers, entered grades, and printed report cards for the global schools of ministry we supported, the Lord refined my ears and my discernment, and he began training my tongue. I learned what it meant to submit when I disagree, which has come in handy many times since then. I learned how to pray instead of gossip. I learned how to trust God's Word over my circumstances and to identify the spirit of shame when it came knocking on the door of my mind. When I wanted to hide, cancel, or retreat, I confessed my sin, one to another, and God healed me. I came closer to him and was honest when I wanted to conceal. I dealt with the difficult emotions that were triggered and allowed God to heal wounds I didn't even know I had. I gave him my yes, time and time again. I submitted the fear of feeling that I might not amount to what I'd hoped and accepted that I might not accomplish or achieve all that was in my heart. I learned to submit my fear to God and turn into faith. I learned to submit my need to control the outcomes of my life to Him, over and over and over again.

Make It Personal

What area of shame have you tried to cover or overproduce in order to keep from dealing with unresolved pain? What area of your life do you need to submit authentically to God and confess to another? James 5:16 tells us to confess our sins to another, and we will be healed. We confess first to God, as I did on the beach that day, and then we begin a process of discipleship with others.

You need to tell your story. What area does the Lord want you to yield to him in a great exchange?

_____

_____

_____

Therefore confess your sins to each other and pray for each other so that you may be healed. The prayer of a righteous person is powerful and effective. (James 5:16)

If we confess our sins, he is faithful and just and will forgive us our sins and purify us from all unrighteousness. (1 John 1:9)

CHAPTER 16

Control versus Surrender

Without choices, there is no real love. This is why God sent his Son, Jesus, to make a way for us to choose him. This day, you get to choose who you will serve. The longer I walk this pilgrimage, the more I realize that while God is extremely patient with us and has more grace than we will ever comprehend, he also gives us the choice because this is the way of love. Until we choose to follow his lead, we will deeply struggle with understanding what it means to trust. *Webster's Dictionary* defines trust as the firm belief in the reliability, truth, ability, or strength of someone or something. We feel the need to control our destiny and make it happen because at the core of our beliefs, fear resides somewhere. We allow cultural lies to speak louder than the small still voice of God that requires our faith. It is impossible to please God without it. We cannot walk the discipleship journey without trusting that God's plans are higher than our own best plans. Often and always, we willingly must choose to lay down our best-made plans, which revolve around our own desires, at the foot of the cross to pick up our crosses and follow God completely.

The character of God is not cruel. Contrary to what the enemy wants us to believe about God, he doesn't hold out on his children. As a parent myself, I desire to give my children the desires of their hearts but not at the expense of being detrimental to their well-being. Often, we long for things that will crush our spiritual vitality and lure us away to lesser gods. As a good Father would, God gives us what we need and sometimes what we want. In time, as we will learn to lay down our desires and discern the core motivations of our hearts, those desires, sanctified by our willingness and sacrifice to lay them down, will rise again, purified through fire, like gold. The good remains, and the dross is burned away.

Perhaps the God-given desires we long for are from him, but they have been tried and tested. The selfish ambition has been burned away, and we are left with the God desires that he placed in our hearts. Unfortunately, this process takes time and trust. It takes following Christ through the crossroads of darkness, where all we can offer are our hands in complete surrender. At the core of mistrust are fragments of this lie that Satan sold Eve. As her daughters, we must recognize it, renounce it, and replace it with the truth.

Eve momentarily believed the lie that God was holding out on her. Do you believe that? What do your actions say about what you believe? Take a moment to renounce the lie that God cannot be trusted. The truth is that God is the foundation of our lives and can be fully trusted as our Creator and a Father who wants the best for our lives. He created us with good purposes in mind, and he wants to release us into those purposes at the right time, not just for our pleasure and fulfillment but for those we will impact positively for God's glory. It is not about us. Our plans are often about us, but that is not the way of the King and his kingdom. The currency of heaven is relationship. God made an effort to put the lonely in families and created his church, the body of believers, to grow in love and the unity of faith. Hebrews reminds us that faith is the substance of things hoped for but not yet seen. That often creates a lot of anxiety, and we work hard at eliminating uncertainty. The road of faith is most certainly uncertain. You must decide to return to your *yes* every time you turn a page in your book of life. The Author has intended a great adventure in the pages of your life, but you'll have to learn to trust him at the turn of every chapter.

My hope for you is that you have been inspired to continue trusting God throughout your entire life. I hope this book inspired your faith and has given you practical handles and courage to keep walking and growing as a disciple, a follower of Jesus who practices his ways. I hope that we have confronted the lie that you are the only one who struggles with your commitment to God and that you are certain now that you are not alone.

THE MOST IMPORTANT YES

I have shared my heart and my life through these pages in the hope that it will remind you that you are in the company of great women of faith who have fought the same fights to shine a light on the pathway, which seems very narrow at times, so that you can find your way. I pray this book has encouraged you to commit to the journey, no matter how long it takes or where it leads you. I pray you will remember the words from this book if you think about abandoning ship because God's path will lead you to confront major giants that have been taunting you for years. I pray you will find the courage to face off with them so that you can continue the narrow path and your walk of faith, as many have done before you. I pray you feel comfort in knowing that you are completely normal in your struggles and that every person of faith worth her salt has walked in your shoes and has confidence that you will make it too.

When you look back and see your footprint as an imprint in the steps of many who have gone before you, you will know that you are on the right path one for you and that many will follow your lead. As we finish this journey together, make a choice in your heart to rededicate your *yes* to God, just as a couple renews their vows after a long journey of ups and downs. Be aware of the shame that is lurking to attack you as you make an agreement with heaven to follow God where he leads. The enemy loves to pray on our weaknesses and to remind us of all the times we've grappled for control and allowed fear to lead us. Remind shame that vulnerability with God and others is its worst nightmare and that you intend on spending the rest of your life exposing its death grip and helping to set others free by telling your story of the road to true freedom in Christ alone!

We overcome by the blood of the Lamb—that is what Jesus did for us—and by the word of our own testimony! This book is a powerful testimony of what God has taught me through my own life experiences; I hope that it will help someone else along this same journey of faith in God. Oh, how I wish I could sit for a cup of coffee and talk with you; this has inspired me to write so that I can do just that. I can sit with you via the words on these pages in places I will never know and be a catalyst for your walk with God. I hope you are recharged and fired up to spend the rest of your life as a living epistle of God's miraculous power and a testimony of the hope found in him.

Make It Personal

As we get close to the end of this journey together, use the blank space below to write a letter to God. This is between you and him. I have boxes of journals with letters to God. I am confident that not one has been wasted because you are reading this book today. It was twenty plus years of journaling that brought me to write to you today. My journal was the place of healing and freedom and a place to express my deepest feelings and thoughts so that I could properly process them with God and others.

Tell Father God where you are, in complete surrender of your plans, before you put this book on the shelf until you reference it again. Let this be the catalyst for many more letters to God in your own journal for years to come.

> Father God,
>
> Thank you for your Son, Jesus, that I can come straight to you authentically today in full confidence that you hear when I call on you. I commit to giving you my yes, again and again, for my entire life. Lead me to the fullness of life that you promised, and lead me into what you had in mind when you wove me together in my mother's womb.

Give him your pain, worry, hopes, and desires right here on these pages. Use a whole blank page, maybe two, for an open dialogue with God. In all your writing, be sure to make space to listen also. Those words will propel you into the next season and give you hope for what is to come!

CHAPTER 17

Trust and Healing

Every meaningful relationship is built on mutual trust. In fact, relationship experts say that without it, there is no authentic relationship.[74] In our case and for the purposes of this book, honoring your yes ultimately requires your trust in God's reliability to copilot your life with you.

God trusts our ability to make a decision to love him back. Real love requires choice, which is why he won't make it for us. He has already made the decision to relentlessly pursue us with the love of a Father who never gives up on us, no matter how far we may think we've run away from him. The question we have to answer is this: will we trust him in return with our whole hearts? It will require us to let go of our need for control and to lean into his strength to help us refrain from reaching for the wheel of our lives, time and again. It is not until we embrace the weakest parts of us that we will experience the strength of God's power in our lives.

I do not enjoy feeling or being weak. In order to grow in our trust of God, it is important to get comfortable with operating in weakness, which is hard for many of us. God likely will call us to do many things in our weaknesses because that is where he shines the best! We cannot take credit for the success that comes through our weakness. Our faith and trust grow in Him as we lean on his understanding and acknowledge all of his ways, not our own.[75]

---

[74] "5 Essential Traits of Lasting Relationships," *Psychology Today*, Oct. 26, 2021, https://www.psychologytoday.com/us/blog/communication-success/202110/5-essential-traits-lasting-relationships.
[75] Proverbs 3:5–6; Isaiah 55:9.

> That is why, for Christ's sake, I delight in weaknesses, in insults, in hardships, in persecutions, in difficulties. For when I am weak, then I am strong. (2 Corinthians 12:10 NIV)

You are guaranteed struggles in this life, as the apostle Peter reminds us in 1 Peter 5:10. If you continually grapple for control every time you feel uncertain, scared, or out of control in your life, the internal battle eventually will wear you out! I speak from experience. Real trust is built in the uncertain times only when you decide to fully let go of your need for control and surrender to God's lead. The small still voice of constant hope and security is best heard in the discipline of silence and solitude.[76] Write down the places where your life feels out of your control, places that cause you fear.

Don't get me wrong; God can get your attention any way he chooses, but the best way to posture our hearts to build trust is with intentionality and the humility to receive the truth from him. We must draw away with the Father on purpose to hear him. I have journal boxes stacked to the ceiling that I have renamed my "trust journey" journals. I have poured my vulnerable soul into the pages of these journals, and they have become trust building blocks in my relationship with God. I have learned to entrust him with the most fragile parts of my heart, including my disappointments, my failures, my pain, my hopes, and my dreams yet to be fulfilled. I often have to recall my first yes, my commitment to a journey of knowing God wherever he led, when I struggle to trust him again with things that stir up fear and anxiety of the unknown.

He already knew me better than I knew myself, and now, it was my turn to get to know him. On the beaches of Fitzroy Island in Australia, I chose to spend the rest of my life getting to know him. That journey has taken me on very different paths than I would have chosen for myself. I allowed the decision to say yes, fully trusting God for the path of my life, to reshape me into his original intent. He knew the deepest desires of my heart better than I did. He knows yours too! The deepest desires of our hearts often are masked with layers of hurt, pain, and trauma. It takes

---

[76] R. Foster, *Celebration of Discipline: The Pathway for Spiritual Growth* (New York; NY: Harper Collins, 2009).

years of intentionality and healing before we can know who we really are and the desires in our hearts that are from God.

Just as a good marriage relationship grows in trust over time and through experiences together, so does our relationship with God, but it won't happen by default. Time is not the only factor that determines the quality of trust in a relationship. Trust is built by taking risks through obedience and seeing God come through for us, time and time again. It requires trusting him with all the broken pieces or weak areas of our lives that we try to hide from others. It is the choice to live with an open heart and hand before God, humbly submitting to his lead.

The mother of our faith, Abraham's wife, Sarah, took a journey, in learning to trust God, that spanned a lifetime of waiting on the promise she wanted the most—a son. She took matters into her own hands a time or two and seemingly lived frustrated during most of her pilgrimage into the desert, after she and her husband obeyed God to leave their homeland. By the time God was ready to deliver her promise, she laughed and thought she was too old for it. Sarah's many disobedient and defiant moments were just as critical in building trust as were the times she obeyed. Sometimes, pain and mistakes are the best teachers. I imagine that every time Sarah insisted on doing things her way, only to end in a disaster—like her maidservant, Hagar, being pregnant with her husband's son—she wished she had trusted God. I have more of those moments than I'd like to recall, but they sure did teach me to not be so hasty in taking matters into my hands and to prayerfully wait on the Lord to fulfill his promises!

He is so good to us that he also promises to turn all things together for the good of those who love him and are called according to his purposes. We see this in the life of Sarah. Even after all the defiance, disobedience, and rebellion, God forgave and blessed her anyway. Aren't you glad that God can use every decision of our lives to get us to where he intends to lead us?[77]

Take a moment to reflect on all the ways you have taken matters into your own hands or blatantly demanded your own way. This is a great place to pause and thank God for relentlessly pursuing you anyhow.

---

[77] Genesis 16.

Selah

I firmly believe that God has had a distinct intent for his creation from the time we were in our mothers' wombs, and that is to reflect his glory in unique ways to the world around us. I had to choose to willingly visit Father God daily in silence and solitude. I pulled away from the noise of life and allowed God to restore the broken places from my inside out, many times. I still do! I can look back over the years and now understand that every journal was a brick of trust, building a history with God. He began to rebuild my life from the inside out and to restore me to his original intent and purpose.

Max Lucado's book *You Are Special* tells the story of a boy who is tired of others placing their expectations on him, as well as placing all the "dots" on him—stickers that indicate their disappointment. He allows their thoughts to bother him until he meets a friend who encourages him to visit the woodcarver. This woodcarver is God, who had the boy's original intent in mind. The woodcarver carefully removes the dots and restores the boy daily as he comes to the workshop to visit.

This is the same with us. We have to visit our Father daily to ensure the "dots" of others' expectations and disappointments don't mar our Father's original vision of what he had in mind.

At some point in our lives, we have to surrender the pride of doing things by ourselves and trust God to get us where he is leading. We all get marred by sin and get beat up along life's journey, but we must make a habit of returning to the Father's workshop for our restoration and a daily yes-I-will-follow-you decision. We will have to confront some of the cultural norms we accepted as God's ways, which are not that at all. They often sound good and are culturally accepted, but we must challenge our belief systems regularly to ensure we are in line with the truth of God's Word that is shaping our lives. We must face off with the three-headed monster of shame, fear, and control that steals our potential and keeps us trapped in the pride of being vulnerable with the one who designed us. Who better to consult for the design for your life than the "woodcarver," Jesus? We must choose to humbly surrender and submit ourselves to God's instruction, the Word of God, and long to hear his whispers to guide our everyday lives as a way of life.

I reached several critical crossroads of surrender that required me to give up the steering wheel of my life, which felt counter to the narrative that we are the masters of our fates. There is some truth in the web of lies that keeps this stronghold in place, so it is important to examine our deeply held beliefs as we reexamine and remodel our thought lives. True love always requires a choice. God does not dictate our every move. He wants our decisions to flow from a solid foundation and relationship with him. This gives us a sensitivity to the leading of his spirit in the direction of our lives.

As I've mentioned, I had to choose to trust God's direction and whispers at the critical crossroads, which were woven together into the tapestry of my life, and you do too!

There were seasons of my "yes, God" moments that felt like I was dying inside. I cried all the way to work at times, wondering if God was punishing me for my wild, adventurous personality or my disobedience. That was such a lie! He loved me enough to teach me his ways in a way that I learned best.

At the Bible college where I worked along my journey back to the narrow road for my life, I talked with the professors, traveling missionaries, and students who often came through the university, and that kept my heart engaged in my day-to-day. One day, a missionary came through from Africa, and he pulled up a chair at my desk. I had a little plaque that my parents had given me that reminded me to *dream* while I was sitting at that desk every day, doing what I thought was less significant at the time. The missionary told me that God saw the desires of my heart and my faithfulness to obey. He said that God was going to make a way for me to go to graduate school debt-free, which I had not even voiced to anyone; it was a secret desire of my heart at that point.

The next year, I was given a full-time job as a recruiter for the graduate school I wanted to attend that would facilitate a debt-free graduate degree. God knew every detail, and as I continued to see him speak and deliver me into the next steps, my trust grew. As I learned to submit myself to his plan, he entrusted me with more responsibility.

When I relocated to Virginia from Florida, it was as if God had already paved the path for me. My dearest friend and spiritual mentor was moving out of her upstairs apartment room in a family home near my university.

THE MOST IMPORTANT YES

After a visit one weekend, I knew that was the place I was to stay and that God had already prepared the way for me. I lived there for two years, and God spoke clearly about things that I later walked out. I lived in a small town close to the university with a gym, a few fast-food restaurants, and the school. There wasn't much going on there, but I learned to discern the Lord's whisper there. He whispered that he would establish me where I was and that I would meet my husband in that sleepy little town.

I had no intention of staying there after graduation or obtaining a "Mrs. degree" while there; in fact, I thought that was insulting at the time. Again, God knew the deepest desires of my heart that I could not articulate at the time. I had dreams of landing a meaningful job with a faith-based nonprofit organization internationally or returning to warmer weather and the islands after graduation. I dreamed of traveling the world again and not going anywhere farther north of where I was. I was designed for the heat, or so I thought. The Lord began to whisper little things to me that challenged and changed my lifestyle. I talked these things over with my roommate, who was a strong Christian leader who was farther down the path than I was, to make sure I was not going crazy or making things up. I obeyed what God was whispering to me in private; this went on for about a year. I heard him whisper things like, *Cook a meal for two*, when I rarely cooked a meal for one. I heard him whisper, more than once, *Do your roommate's laundry*, and *Do more than your fair share*.

One of the most humiliating things I did in pure obedience and learning to trust was to try on a wedding dress when I didn't even have a boyfriend. I had vowed secretly to never try on a wedding dress before it was time, so I denied what I'd heard for weeks. Finally, I confessed what I'd heard to my roommate, who dragged me to the wedding dress store that happened to be strategically placed across from the gym, where I later met my future husband a year later. As I tried on that dress, I felt the Holy Spirit whisper to me that my husband was there, but he would always be my first love. Now over a decade into marriage, I have learned that keeping Jesus your first love is the key to any thriving relationship.

I had such a poor track record; I'd never had a boyfriend for more than two weeks, let alone a lifetime. One year later, I was minding my business in my boot-camp exercise class when a gentleman caught my eye, and apparently, I caught his. I wasn't interested, but our talking on the elliptical eventually led us to a nondate at Tropical Smoothie after a workout—we walked right past the dress store where God had spoken to me. Six months later, we were engaged, and I was terrified but at peace. This was messing with the plans I had in mind. Logically, I did not think I was a short-engagement type of person, but I felt the Holy Spirit leading, so I followed. I learned to just keep walking, even if it didn't make sense and it wasn't my plan. The truth is that it scared me, and I fought to keep from running from the relationship many times.

Fast-forward a year: as newlyweds, God spoke to both of us separately about moving to the Washington, DC, metro area, which was a place I'd never imagined living. I prayed that God would send me to the Nations on a mission for his purposes with a nonprofit, meeting needs in the community. I found myself in the concrete jungle of the most politically charged city in the nation, which did not seem to fit who I was. This was not my dream, but I gave God my yes and kept following.

Three years later, God spoke to my husband first about children. I simply wasn't ready yet again. I wrestled with God, followed my husband's lead, and entrusted my yes to Jesus to the call of motherhood. I was terrified but had chosen a long time ago to give him my yes so that was settled. My decision to say yes to God's leading in my life has helped me to make the decisions I have wrestled with in life and still does. I'd already made up my mind to trust him with my yes. I needed to do a lot of introspection in my heart and renewing of my mind around having children. These were all fears that God helped me break down and get his perspective on as I surrendered and replaced those thoughts. I gave God my yes, and while it was difficult, it was the best decision I ever made.

I would like to tell you that my yes got easier with my son and younger daughter to follow, but it did not. It was still in a wrestling match as I chose again to give him my yes with complete trust three times. I have found when you stand at the door of destiny, the spirit of fear is right there too. It appears much bigger than it really is and requires courage to get to the root of what is causing so much internal resistance to following. I have learned to see those moments as invitations to overcome.

Now, I cannot believe I get to be my children's mother; I cannot believe how much they have changed me for the better. I see why God wanted them here because they are true gifts to the world. Life is never just about us, and God always has multiple generations in mind. They were sent on assignment from heaven to show God's love in their own uniqueness. I had to surrender many dreams and desires a thousand times over. Slowly, he has made a way to see those come to fruition in totally different ways than I ever imagined. I gave God my trust when I said yes to our relationship, and he has proved trustworthy over and over again. It has not happened in my timing or fast enough at times, but in the waiting and trusting, I have become more like him even in all my imperfections. I think that is the point. And I still have a long way to go.

Trust is risky yet the most rewarding experience we can have as humans. What is there not to trust about our Creator who formed us in our mothers' wombs, numbered the hairs on our heads, and breathed life into our formless bodies? His design and leading is likely far more fulfilling than what we can muster in our own strength. We began in the heart of God. He entrusts us with the free will to give our hearts back to him. He designed us to trust and live in loving union as one. As we choose to yield to God's ways, we shine his light brighter and brighter to the world around us. In loving union with God, we can do all things, as he enables us with courage and strength. Without him, we will be limited by our own understanding, perceived abilities, and human limitations. As we learn to trust God in the hard things, the world around us takes note that our strength comes from a different place and is not rooted in our own abilities to perform and rely on ourselves. That is not God's way. The world's way is to trust ourselves to make the plan and create the "perfect" life, but the true trust is built in surrendering our lives to God's lead.

Trust is strengthened with every yes as we follow God's lead and build confidence that he really does know how to lead us best. Mary Magdalene trusted God to empower her to give the message of Jesus's Resurrection to her brothers, as the first woman evangelist. Phoebe trusted God to counter culture and assist the apostle Paul in carrying the gospel to planted churches as a woman leader in a time when that was unpopular. Deborah decided to trust God in leading men to war. Priscilla decided to colead with her husband and strengthen churches alongside the apostle Paul for future generations. These women trusted

God and made a way for us today. We stand on their shoulders and continue to allow God to write our stories. Someday, other women will read the stories of our lives and be encouraged to be strong and courageous and to trust God's lead too.[78]

Make It Personal

Take a moment to ask God the following questions. Remember that you can hear from God! He speaks in many ways, and journaling is a way to help you hear from God. I have found that asking questions and practicing silent prayer is one of the most powerful tools we have. Take five to ten minutes before moving on to your day to silence the inner hustle, and ask God these questions. Write down what you see, hear, or sense. Be sure it aligns with God's character and his Word. Share with a trusted spiritual leader or friend in your life.

Father, are there any areas of my life in which I have withheld my trust? If yes, what?

_____

_____

_____

Take a moment to ask God's forgiveness for not trusting him in that area. Write down the lie so you can see it. Take a moment to write, "I break agreement with the lie that _____"

_____

_____

_____

---

[78] L. Cunningham & D. J. Hamilton, *Why Not Women?* (Seattle, WA: YWAM Publishing, 2000).

Ask Father God what the truth is about that area in which you've struggled to trust him. Hold on to whatever he shares with you. Take a moment to write it down here. Reference it often when you struggle to trust him in that area again.

_____

_____

CHAPTER 18

The Waiting and Reward

Have you ever been around children when it was near their birthdays or Christmas? In my house, my children begin asking about their birthdays at least a month ahead of time, and every day, they ask me the same question: "How much longer do I have to wait?" Children have no muscles for patience or a grit for waiting for anything. Delayed gratification, self-control, and time have no relevance to them. Kids naturally want everything now!

Unfortunately, it was not until I started raising my own children that I realized how childish I could act with God when it came to waiting for things I'd prayed about and desired. The apostle Paul instructed the church of Corinth to essentially grow up, comparing the immaturity he saw there to children. Man, did I ever act childish when it came to waiting on God to answer my prayers or to speak to me about something I longed to know on a more specific timeline. The apostle Paul said it best:

> When I was a child, I talked like a child, I thought like a child, I reasoned like a child. When I became a man, I put the ways of childhood behind me. (1 Corinthians 13:11)

The ability to wait patiently and resist the urge to take matters into your own hands is a sign of maturity, as it is in your spiritual life. As my children have grown developmentally, they are able to wait more patiently; they even save money for things they desire or deny themselves an impulse buy. This takes self-discipline and delaying gratification, which are necessary for a life that honors God in a microwave culture of "I want it now!"

When we learn to trust God with our lives and surrender our wills and waiting to him, it becomes easier to trust God's timing. It will become easier to discern what drives you forward on something you desire or whether it's the Holy Spirit's prompting that is time to move ahead. As a type-A, driven personality, waiting has been the hardest discipline of my life. As I've learned to trust God's leading, and I've yielded to his voice in my life, he has proven himself trustworthy. I have discovered, during the wait, that *he* is actually the great reward, not the thing I thought I desired the most. During the wait, we often discover contentment with the life that God has given us.

Given some of my spiritual giftings, it is not uncommon for me to see or sense things ahead of time, yet my timing is years off. There were times when the Lord spoke to me in dreams of future events, and I mistakenly thought it would be tomorrow, only for them to manifest themselves years later. As women who like to execute a plan swiftly, our critical mission will be to hone in on the discipline of waiting on God and not rushing ahead. When we are so focused on the outcome and completely miss the process of what God is doing, we are sure to make poor decisions. The great matriarch of our faith, Sarah, rushed ahead of God's timing, and it caused strife in her family and produced consequences for generations. We must realize that waiting well doesn't impact only us but future generations to come. We are not exempt from the same test of waiting on God in our own generation.

The best practical thing I've found to help me in the waiting is to journal my emotions to God. I tell the Lord what and how I'm feeling. He can handle it, and he already knows! I put the impatient, hurried soul on paper and wait to hear from the Lord on it. I actively listen once I've written down what is on my heart and mind. I then write down what he tells me, which rarely has a specific timetable to put into my strategic planning. The weightiness of his words, as the great reward himself, calms my mind and gives me hope. He always assures me that I can trust him with my every concern. You, too, can trust him with whatever door you're waiting to open! He is a good Father, and he desires what is best for your life. Sometimes, even we do not know what is best for our lives, we must surrender the impatience to God. In the waiting, the Lord can sift through the deepest motivations of our hearts, and we will realize that he is the reward, not the outcome of the thing for which we are waiting.

In my last year of graduate school, I finally noticed a deeper desire for companionship in this long journey of life. I was also at the place of accepting that might not be God's will for me. I am a work in progress on self-compassion and I finally allowed myself to be honest with God about the deepest desires of my heart. I allowed my soul to speak, and I listened. God already knew the truth about how he wired me, and he sorted through the deepest desires of my heart, although they had been buried beneath pain and disappointment. That led to many steps of obedience that year until I was ready to walk the aisle and marry my husband.

Why would God prepare me for that moment a year before meeting my husband, followed by 365 days of silence on the matter? I have no idea, but I do know that I learned to trust the Word of the Lord in faith. My confidence to hear God's voice grew in the silence. I am sure that Moses felt similarly when God told him to lead the children of Israel out of Egyptian slavery, and they wandered in the desert for forty years. I am sure Moses wondered if he had heard God correctly in the wait.[79] God told me in a local wedding shop that my husband was there. God's "here" was spot-on, but it took some time to understand what he meant. Jeremy and I met at the gym across the street from that local wedding shop a year from the time I tried on a wedding dress in complete obedience to what I heard him tell me to do.

Later in life, I took many job assignments that would last years, even though I knew they were leading me somewhere else in my future. I struggled to be faithful every day until God revealed what those assignments were teaching me for my future. I suspect God has you on a similar journey and none of us have arrived. He longs to meet you in those assignments as you are faithful to what he has put in front of you right now.

I have a dozen other stories of learning to trust God and surrendering in the wait. I have learned that a day is like a thousand years to the Lord.[80] Our timing and his timing are not the same. Anything he calls us to wait for will be better than we could have ever made happen on our own. If

---

[79] Genesis 14.
[80] Psalm 90:4.

the mother of our faith, Sarah, were talking to us now, I bet she'd tell us that the wait is well worth it. In the waiting and surrendering to God's timing, God transforms us and our desires to align with his for our lives. God began to prepare my heart long before I met Jeremy for what was the second biggest decision of my adult life, after the decision to follow Christ.

Years may pass between a promise that God speaks to you and its fruition. Though it takes time, commit your heart to wait on it![81] In the process of the wait, open your hands and your heart in surrender to God's timing. Surrender all of you, and allow God to prepare you for what you're waiting for. He is the great reward, not the promise itself. Who we become in the waiting is far more important than the promise itself. We have an opportunity to grow in our faith and grow in confidence that God is a promise-keeper! Surrender your ideas about what you think or how you think it will be. God is good, and he knows you better than you know yourself.

What are you waiting for in this season? I believe the Lord wants to speak and remind you of his promises over your life regarding the thing you've been waiting for before you close this book. Every time you think about that unfulfilled promise, I want you to remember some of the key take-aways from my journey that will help spur you onward in yours. God is not finished writing your story, and he cares deeply for the things that matter to you. Take some time to hear from God. Use the journal section below, and ponder what he says in your heart, no matter how long it takes.

Mary held on to the words the angel spoke to her for thirty-three years, and then she realized that her son was truly the Messiah. Like Mary, Jesus's mother, you may wonder if you heard correctly, but remember that God's timing is not your timing. I have found that God's promises and his timing is not just about us. It is often about future generations and the people he will impact through our lives, sister! Hannah's wait for her son, Samuel, would impact generations of Kings and a nation. Elizabeth's yes to wait, birthed a forerunner for the gospel through her son, John. Deborah's yes to take Barak alongside her, won a battle. Priscilla's yes to business allowed she and her husband to advance the gospel through resourcing the vision. There is a generation, a community of people, and a family that your yes to wait is counting on. You may never know the full impact of your wait

---

[81] Habakkuk 2:3–4.

but God does. Our struggles and tears pave the way for others to walk a clearer and narrower path that will lead to life. His ways are higher than even your brightest ideas; therefore, wait for his!

Make It Personal

What are you waiting for in this season? Write it out.

_____

_____

_____

_____

Is that what you truly want? Is anything you wrote down coming from a false sense of self, or are they genuine desires you believe that God put there?

_____

_____

_____

_____

Read aloud Isaiah 55:8–9 (below), and write it out. Submit those thoughts to God in surrender of those dreams in your heart.

_____

_____

_____

_____

> For my thoughts are not your thoughts, neither are your ways my ways," declares the Lord. As the heavens are higher than the earth, so are my ways higher than your ways and my thoughts more than your thoughts.

Pray the following scripture out loud, and make a recommitment to trust God with your story.

> Wait on the Lord: be of good courage, and he shall strengthen thine (my) heart: wait, I say, on the Lord. (Psalms 27:14)

Don't let this be the end of your intimate conversations with God but merely a catalyst that encouraged you and breathed faith into your heart for your own story with God.

Printed in the USA
CPSIA information can be obtained
at www.ICGtesting.com
LVHW041008100824
787869LV00001B/195